THIS BOOK BELONGS TO

Camilo

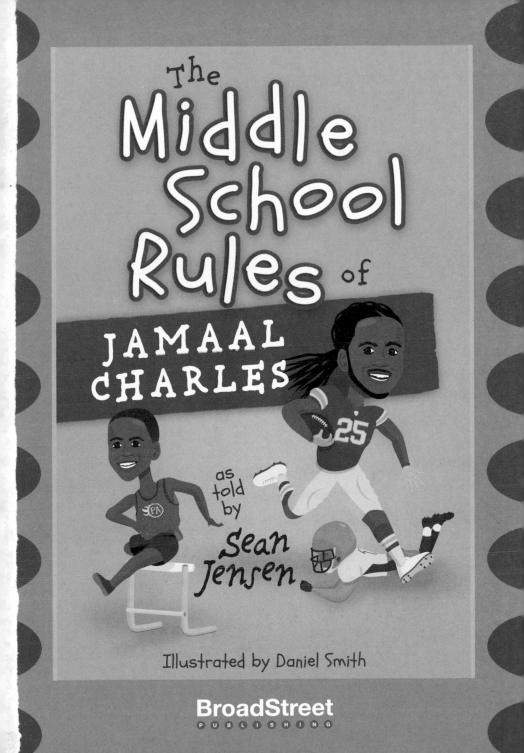

The Middle School Rules of

JAMAAL CHARLES

as told by

Sean Jensen

Illustrated by Daniel Smith

BroadStreet
PUBLISHING

BroadStreet Publishing Group LLC
Racine, Wisconsin, USA
broadstreetpublishing.com

Middle School Rules of Jamaal Charles

ISBN 978-1-4245-5300-6 (hard cover)
ISBN 978-1-4245-5301-3 (e-book)

Illustrated by Daniel Smith.
Back cover photo courtesy of The Kansas City Chiefs / Steve Sanders.

Cover and interior design by Garborg Design Works I garborgdesign.com
Editorial services provided by Ginger Garrett I gingergarrett.com
and Michelle Winger I literallyprecise.com

Printed in China.

17 18 19 20 21 22 23   7 6 5 4 3 2 1

ACKNOWLEDGMENTS

from Jamaal Charles

I want to thank my whole family for helping me put this book together. I want to thank my friends who supported me, my coaches, and my teachers. And, of course, my Port Arthur community.

Also, thank you to Coach Brown and Drew for inspiring me to pursue this goal of writing a book about my childhood.

I couldn't have done this without my wife Whitney's support.

from Sean Jensen

I thank God for all he has done in my life.

I thank my wife Erica for her continual support, and my kids, Elijah and Zarah, for inspiring me.

I also want to thank Ted Crews of the Kansas City Chiefs for making the initial connection and Andrew Kessler of Athletes First for passionately working to tell Jamaal's story in the most authentic way possible.

Lastly, I want to thank Daniel Smith and our team at BroadStreet Publishing for their professionalism and expertise.

INTRODUCTION

Dear Reader,

I want to inspire you, in case any of you are going through what I did.

There is light at the end of the tunnel. Don't feel that you don't have a chance in this world.

We need to ask for help so we can get help in every part of our life: education, sports, or anything else you want to do.

There are resources. Don't be afraid to ask for help from your parents, family members, teachers, or coaches.

There is plenty of help in this world.

I hope you enjoy my story.

Jamaal Charles

Jamaal

Jamaal with his mother and brothers

Jamaal's Grandma

Jamaal and Cal Jones

5

FOREWORD

As a native of Port Arthur, I heard rumors of this kid who might be the next superstar from Southeast Texas. I, along with my law partner and our wives, attended Jamaal's next high school football game. On his first carry from scrimmage, Jamaal ran 65 yards for a touchdown.

The crowd was going crazy and I could see that he was fast—no, really fast! Unfortunately, there was a yellow flag on the field, and his touchdown was negated by a holding penalty. Everyone was upset, and I could tell that Jamaal was really disappointed. Shortly after the penalty, I learned everything I needed to know about Jamaal's true character.

The head football coach was yelling at Jamaal's teammate for getting the penalty and costing the team a touchdown. But Jamaal approached his teammate, who had his head hanging down, and gave his teammate an encouraging slap on his shoulder pads. I could not tell what Jamaal said to him; however, the once disappointed teammate picked up his head, and they ran back into the huddle together.

The very next play, the coach decided to hand Jamaal the ball again... and he ran 75 yards for a touchdown! Everyone could see that Jamaal was a talented football player. But I could see that Jamaal was an outstanding person.

When Jamaal had to experience very difficult life challenges, he stayed positive, encouraged the people around him, and fought hard to succeed. Privately, Jamaal and I have talked about many of the difficulties he has encountered, both professionally and personally. While most people see Jamaal as a gifted football superstar, I see him as a humble person constantly seeking guidance to become a better person.

I have watched Jamaal mature from a very passive kid to a God-fearing man and devoted father. Although I am not Jamaal's biological father, I am proud to call him one of my sons. As you read Jamaal's life story, I hope that you will learn that his football success was not a guarantee. What I hope you discover is that Jamaal's true success is the person (not the player) he has become.

Before every game throughout his entire NFL career, we have prayed together and given thanks to God for allowing Jamaal to become an overcomer. While I believe Jamaal will one day be inducted into the Pro Football Hall of Fame, I hope his off-the-field traits allow others to experience his true "GREATNESS."

May many blessings come,

Attorney James E. Payne
Port Arthur, Texas

TABLE OF CONTENTS

Chapter 1

The Refrigerator

O n December 27th, two days after Christmas, on a frigid and foggy day in Port Arthur, Texas, Jamaal RaShaad Charles enters the world. His childhood will be full of surprises, but the first one belongs to his mom.

He's a boy!

His mom Sharon already has three boys, and she wants a little girl. But Jamaal is a boy, and he's huge! Weighing 10 pounds at birth, about two-and-a-half pounds heavier than an average baby, Jamaal immediately receives an unflattering nickname.

Relatives jokingly call him *Refrigerator*. He's big!

They say everything's bigger in Texas so he fits right in. Texas is the second-largest state in the United States. When oil boomed in the early 1900s, Port Arthur became one of the mighty state's biggest little towns. Major oil refineries were built there, taking advantage of access to railroads and a canal from Sabine Lake to the Gulf of Mexico.

THE REFRIGERATOR

Port Arthur is 91 miles east of Houston, near the Louisiana border. The population was 900 people in 1900 and over 50,000 by 1930! By the 1950s, Port Arthur is one of the central points of oil in the entire world plus the birthplace of music legend Janis Joplin, former Texas governor Allan Shivers, Super Bowl and NCAA champion football coach Jimmy Johnson, and arguably one of the greatest female athletes, Babe Zaharias.

Port Arthur produces a lot of oil and plenty of amazing people. But when the oil industry starts to decline so does Port Arthur. Shops close and crime increases. By the 1990s, the town has one of the highest crime rates in the U.S.

Port Arthur has changed a lot in a century. Jamaal likes his hometown, though.

Jamaal's dad is around, but he does not have a major impact on his life. His brothers, though, are always nearby, and they are all older: Darryl by six years, ShanDerrick by four years, and Kevin by three years. Jamaal's mom raises him and his brothers with the help of her parents, Mazell and Oscar Miller.

Jamaal clings to his mom. Though family is always around, Jamaal never leaves his mom's side, not when she goes to the store, not when she plays cards, not even when she sleeps.

Another nickname emerges.

"Stop being so attached to your momma!" one cousin yells at Jamaal.

"Let your momma breathe!" another cousin says to him.

"Why are you such a momma's boy?" a third cousin asks Jamaal.

Jamaal does not answer.

Even when he learns to speak, Jamaal does not have much to say. And though he has more than 50 cousins, Jamaal keeps to himself—and near his mom.

Chapter 2

Grandma's House

Jamaal moves several times with his mom, but they often end up at the home of his mom's father Oscar and mother Mazell. They live on the corner of 17th Street and Galveston Avenue.

The house is beige with brown trim and a wooden porch.

There's grass in the back and on each side. But the kids like to play in the grass along Galveston Avenue. Ms. Cora, the neighbor, fusses at them all the time. She dislikes balls banging against the side of her house or one of the cousins eating her kumquats—a small citrus fruit—in the front garden. The grass is a better place to play because no one fusses at them there.

Jamaal and other children call Oscar by his nickname, Paw Paw, and everyone knows Mazell as Grandma.

Grandma's house has three bedrooms and seven rules.

GRANDMA'S HOUSE RULES
No fighting.
No lying.
No cussing (saying naughty words).
Finish your food.
Be in the house when the street lights come on.
Respect your elders by answering them with "sir" and "ma'am."
Anything Grandma says is a rule.

Everyone respects the seventh rule.

Paw Paw works as a painter at the shipyard. Grandma works as a custodian at Thomas Jefferson High School. Together they provide for their nine children plus the nephews, nieces, cousins, and neighbors who regularly come into their care.

Grandma is used to being around a lot of family; she is the second-youngest of 16 kids herself.

People flock to Grandma's house because some say they can feel the warmth and love there. Grandma does not believe in strangers.

Once, a man selling encyclopedias door-to-door stops by her house about a half hour before dinnertime. It's 90 degrees outside, and he wears a suit. Sweat soaks through his white dress shirt and suit jacket.

Grandma insists he enter her home for a drink of water.

"That sounds like a big inconvenience, ma'am," the salesman says.

"It is no worry at all," Grandma says, opening up the door all the way and extending her arms to invite him into the living room.

Grandma quickly shuffles to the kitchen to get the salesman a glass of water with ice, and she asks him where he's from.

"I'm from Beaumont," he says, referring to a town about 20 miles away.

"We have family in Beaumont," Grandma says, as she returns with the glass of water.

The salesman tilts the glass and gulps it all down.

"Oh, my!" Grandma says. "You were *very* thirsty. I'll bet you're hungry, too. Beans are cooking on the stove and pork chops are about to come out of the oven. You must join my family for dinner."

It isn't a question.

This sort of thing happens all the time at Grandma's house.

But Grandma does not tolerate wild children in her house or yard. If you do not listen to her or abide by her seven rules, you are sent away.

One neighbor boy bounces a basketball in the living room after he is told by a grownup to stop. Grandma directs him toward the front door.

"Go home," she tells him. "You're not listening to grown folks."

A few days later, the neighbor boy returns and pulls aside Jamaal's brother ShanDerrick.

"Can you ask your grandma if I can come back to the house?"

"No, you better ask her yourself!" ShanDerrick replies. "You're not getting me in trouble with Grandma!"

The neighbor boy slinks toward the living room, where

Grandma is reading her Bible full of highlights and folded pages.

"I'm sorry, Ms. Miller," he says sheepishly. "I promise to listen better."

She nods and offers a small smile.

Staying at Grandma's house also means your homework is done before you play outside after school, you are inside when the streetlights come on, and your plate has no food left over—including field peas, which *all* the kids dislike.

Except for Jamaal.

When Grandma gets up to get a second plate of food, Jamaal's cousins load their peas on his plate, and Jamaal eats them all up.

There's one problem in Grandma's house.

There's only one bathroom. It's always a race to reach it first in the morning or else you might have to hold off using it for a *long* time. After he's potty-trained, Jamaal often beats his brothers and cousins to the bathroom.

Chapter 3

Ja-Millie

Jamaal is an easy target for his brothers and cousins. He is the youngest so he cannot physically defend himself, and he does not verbally defend himself.

They pick on him for a couple reasons: he cries when he gets mad, and his name is funny.

"Jamaal is a girly name," Jamaal's older brother Kevin says. "I'm going to call you Ja-Millie."

The cousins crack up.

"That's a good one!" one of them says. "Ja-Millie is perfect."

Jamaal cries, which only makes his brothers and cousins even more relentless. The meanness stings him even more when it comes from relatives.

When Jamaal can walk and talk, his mom is not around as much because of work. Sometimes she works multiple jobs to support her boys. Jamaal gravitates toward Grandma. She defends him, and she demands the kids stop calling him names.

"Don't call my baby Ja-Millie!" Grandma says loudly, before shooing everyone away while she consoles Jamaal.

The kids hurry away, exploding into laughter when they are far enough away from Grandma.

Instead of playing games and sports, Jamaal stays near Grandma.

The times Jamaal is picked on most is after school when Grandma sheds her work clothes, puts on a pink flowered cotton robe, and naps on the living room couch.

Jamaal's brothers and cousins always go back to calling him Ja-Millie. They pick on him until he bursts into tears. Because he does not want to wake up Grandma, Jamaal runs away to a bedroom or the front porch. He runs anywhere that leads away from his tormentors.

Jamaal's brothers and cousins label him a cry-baby. They do not let him tag along to play at nearby parks or friends' houses because he's so much younger.

So Jamaal spends a lot of time with Grandma. She loves everyone but pays special attention to Jamaal. A Christian woman, Grandma repeatedly shares a message with him when he's picked on too much.

GRANDMA'S RULE
"Don't listen to them," she says. "Listen to God."

Jamaal goes to church, and he knows there is a God. But he does not feel a relationship with God yet. Still, Grandma's words and hugs always make him feel better.

If Grandma trusts God, he thinks maybe he should too.

Chapter 4

Saturday Chores

At Grandma and Paw Paw's house, Saturday mornings do not start with cartoons and cookies.

PAW PAW'S RULE:

"There are no free rides," he says. "Everyone must do their part."

Any girls staying at the house wax the floors and do other inside chores. All the boys staying at the house pick up leaves and mow the grass. Fortunately for the boys, the front never needs mowing. They've worn out the grass so it cannot grow!

Neither can flowers. Grandma tries to make her own garden like her neighbor Ms. Cora, but all the kids in

SATURDAY CHORES

1
2
3
4
5
6

her yard trample budding plants while playing sports and hide-and-seek.

Why would kids want to stay at Grandma's on Friday night?

After chores, Grandma treats the children to biscuits, maple syrup and fig preserves, all made from scratch—meaning she mixes ingredients using her own recipes. The biscuits are big and fluffy, and the maple syrup is thick and sweet!

If it rains, the kids sometimes play a card game indoors called smutt-smutt. The last person holding the most cards lets everyone else put powder on their face!

But the kids usually pick a sport outdoors. There's a rollaway basketball rim in the garage. Football games take place on the street, in the yard, or at a nearby park. And they race around Grandma's house. They have to run relays a lot because there are so many cousins.

The race starts right outside Grandma's house, on the corner of Galveston and 17th. The first sprinter heads to 18th Street, the second sprinter to Richmond Avenue, the third down Richmond toward 17th, and the anchor back to Galveston and 17th.

Years later, Uncle Kent insists on joining a race.

"Back in the day," he says, "I was the fastest kid around."

Jamaal and Kevin roll their eyes.

Uncle Kent is over 40 years old, and he does not sprint anymore. Still, he lines up with Jamaal, Kevin, and Keithie for a sprint to the end of the block.

Jamaal does not worry about Uncle Kent or even Keithie. He believes his brother Kevin will be his toughest challenger.

The boys dash off, and Uncle Kent immediately falls behind. For some reason, he reaches out and tries to grab Keithie, but he misses.

Uncle Kent tumbles and crashes to the street. He tears his shirt, and skins his arms and knees.

Kevin barely beats Jamaal, and they do not understand what happened to Uncle Kent until the others explain. The kids try to contain their laughter but the adults who are watching cannot.

"Go clean yourself up, old man!" one of them says.

"I'm not old!" Uncle Kent replies.

Jamaal sees that sometimes adults get picked on too.

Chapter 5

Killer Millers

Athletes abound in Jamaal's family:

Michael Miller, who was Grandma and Paw Paw's oldest child, was one of the first African American sports stars at Thomas Jefferson High School in the 1970s.

Sharon Miller was a standout long and triple jumper.

Arlene Miller starred in track.

Bruce Miller was an All-State running back on Thomas Jefferson's state runner-up football team.

Graylin Johnson played football at the University of Texas.

Terry Miller joined the Cleveland Indians farm system but did not pursue a professional career.

Evelyn Miller was the "Ping Pong" queen.

John Miller starred in track.

When Jamaal's mother was young, she and her siblings dominated sports, too. They played everything from baseball to football to basketball to track and field.

The family earns a nickname: The Killer Millers!

When Jamaal is five, his mom and Uncle Robert coach his t-ball team because they know the sport so well. Jamaal's team does not lose a game. Other teams accuse the Millers of cheating because the team roster is filled with relatives.

When he is six, Jamaal plays flag football with his cousins, including Keisha and Dustin.

Because he's a big six-year-old, Jamaal plays all the positions

on offense and defense. His cousin RaShonta, also known as Tae-Tae, plays quarterback.

Jamaal's favorite part of football is jumping across the line of scrimmage and drilling the other team's quarterback or running back. He cares more about tackles than touchdowns.

Snap!

He loves the sound of the flag snapping off an opponent's belt. That means the play is over.

Always full of energy, Jamaal plays at a different speed than most of the other kids. Sometimes his mom yells at him, "Jamaal, calm down!"

Jamaal's team wins every game by five or six touchdowns. They reach the championship game against the Cobras, a team from the nearby town of Orange.

Jamaal's team does not score easily against the Cobras. In fact, at halftime, they are only up by one touchdown. The Cobras' best player spins through two defenders to score one touchdown on offense. Then, on defense, he makes all his team's tackles.

Jamaal does not know what to make of the Cobra player. Since Jamaal can keep up with his older brothers and cousins, he knows he is fast. But he's never come across another kid his age who is faster than he is!

Could it be possible?

The Cobras have the ball for the game's final possession. Jamaal, lined up at linebacker, guesses a pass is coming, but the Cobra running back runs straight at him—and past him.

The Cobras are the champions.

As his cousins line up to shake the Cobras' hands, Jamaal stays on the sideline and cries. His mom comes over to him.

"What's wrong, Jamaal?" she asks.

"That kid was fast," he says between sobs, "and I couldn't catch him!"

"I'm sorry to hear that," Mom says, "but it's time to shake their hands."

"I don't want to," Jamaal says, folding his arms and stiffening up his back.

MOM'S RULE
"You can't win all the time. Winning or losing makes you a better person, so always be a good sport."

Jamaal knows his mom is right, and he unfolds his arms. He then trots toward the middle of the field and shakes hands with the Cobras.

Afterwards, Jamaal is still bitter about the loss, but ice cream on the way home makes things a little better.

Chapter 6

Making Disciples

Children have some choices in Grandma's house: which games to play, what snacks to eat, even when to sleep. But attending Zion Hill Missionary Baptist Church on Sundays is not optional. For Grandma, there is no excuse to miss church or show up late—not being tired, not oversleeping, and not playing in an athletic event.

Even if the game is out of town.

Once Arlene and Sharon have a multi-day softball tournament in Louisiana. But Grandma demands they come home Saturday night  and then attend church Sunday morning. After church they can return to Louisiana to play their softball games.

Grandma wakes everyone up at 7:30 a.m. They all take turns washing up in one bathroom. Sunday School—where adults teach children about religion—starts at 9:30 a.m. Grandma requires all children to attend Sunday School.

Or else.

After Sunday School, there's *more* church. The morning service starts at 10:45, and the afternoon service starts at 3.

Grandma sometimes insists they all go to the evening service after dinner too.

As she dishes out breakfast, Grandma often cites her favorite Bible verse: "I can do all things through Christ who gives me strength." (Philippians 4:13)

She reminds the children about the secret to having a strong family.

GRANDMA'S RULE

"A family that prays together," she says, "stays together. Don't ever forget that."

One Sunday morning, a cousin who has never stayed at Grandma's refuses to get up. Kevin pokes him in the ribs.

"Hey, Grandma doesn't play when it comes to church," he says. "You better get up or else you'll catch a whooping."

Zion Hill is not a big church. It has 14 pews in two rows. About 100 folks can squeeze into the building, and many members serve in multiple ways.

Paw Paw is a deacon, and Grandma is a deaconess. These are positions of leadership in a church. Other family—including Uncle Kent on drums and Aunt Evelyn as director—make up the choir. Cousin Keisha sings beautifully, and she sometimes brings members to tears.

Fall asleep or act up in church, and Grandma might twist your ear, or worse yet, take you outside for a spanking.

"Pay attention," she says. "You need the Word."

But the children's favorite part is leaving church for the 12-minute drive back to Grandma's house.

Chapter 7

Sunday Dinner

Grandma's favorite tradition is Sunday Dinner. She usually feeds between 20 and 30 family members and friends. At holidays, she feeds about 80 people!

To cook for that many people means Grandma starts the process early. In fact, she starts it the day before. On Saturday, she starts the pork roast and sides such as collard greens, black-eyed peas and okra.

By late Sunday afternoon, Grandma's feast features oven-baked and smothered ribs, homemade mac-and-cheese, cornbread, yams, mashed potatoes, fried chicken, and assorted pies.

And, of course, her biscuits.

But do not even try to sneak a taste of something or hang around the kitchen. Once, Jamaal's cousin Little Mike, who *loves* food, was near the kitchen counter.

"Boy, go away!" Grandma yells as she swings a spoon at him. "The food ain't ready. Go sit down until I tell you it's time to eat!"

The small dining room seats only six, so folks eat in the living room, on the front porch, in the backyard, or anywhere there's a spot to rest and enjoy Grandma's cooking.

The food is delicious—Grandma is the family's best cook, after all. But what makes the tradition special is not the food. It is the jokes, smiles, and bonds between family and friends.

Jamaal never actually sees Grandma make a plate for herself. If she is not in the kitchen preparing or dishing out food, she is chatting and hugging visitors.

Nothing brings Grandma more joy than hosting Sunday Dinners at home.

Chapter 8

Acting Out

Jamaal is competitive with his brothers and cousins. Since he is one of the youngest and one of the smallest, Jamaal can't beat them in sports. One activity he can beat them in is video games. The boys crowd around the living room television and play John Madden Football, NBA Jam, and Tomb Raider.

But video games bring out the worst in Jamaal... and his brother ShanDerrick. They yell when a football play does not go according to plan. Sometimes they throw the controller.

"The game is fake," Mom reminds them.

Jamaal falls on the ground and cries.

"Boy, get off the ground and stop crying!" Mom tells him.

Jamaal is not only crying because of video game disappointments. His brothers and cousins still pick on him because he whines and cries.

At home, Jamaal endures the name-calling and bullying. But at school, Jamaal acts out and misbehaves. By second grade, most students learn to read. But Jamaal struggles to keep up with classmates. They make fun of him.

"What's wrong with you?" Rita asks him. "That's a picture of a dog, so why are you saying *door*?"

Jamaal struggles to pronounce words and string them together. As he falls behind, he decides to crack jokes. He can get others to laugh *with* him, not at him. He becomes a class clown.

He disrupts the class by making funny faces and saying silly things.

The teacher, Ms. Regan, does not appreciate foolishness in her classroom. She threatens to call Jamaal's home.

"Call my grandma then," Jamaal dares her. "Go ahead and call her!"

"Oooh..." several students near him say under their breath.

Ms. Regan leaves the chalkboard and heads toward her desk in the back. Without saying a word, she looks at her notebook, picks up her red phone, and dials a number.

"Yes, is this Mrs. Miller?" Ms. Regan says. "I am sorry to bother you on this lovely afternoon, but Jamaal is being disruptive in class, and I thought you might want to know."

Ms. Regan pauses, nodding her head.

"Oh, you're going to come to the school *now*?" Ms. Regan says. "Well, see you shortly."

Jamaal thinks Ms. Regan is not serious.

But 10 minutes later...

Grandma storms through the classroom door, holding a long tree branch. She looks mad.

Jamaal sinks into his seat.

"Get up here, Jamaal!" Grandma says.

Jamaal looks around. He wishes there were another boy with that name to save him. But he knows Grandma is there for him, and he knows the switch is not for decoration.

Jamaal slowly walks toward the front of the class. The other students are wide-eyed at what is taking place. When he gets near Grandma, she starts to whip him with the switch and adds, "Don't you act like a clown in class! You know better."

Grandma embarrasses Jamaal. He does know better.

Later, before dinner, Grandma pulls Jamaal aside

"I know school is tough," she tells him. "But that's no excuse to bother your teacher."

GRANDMA'S RULE
"Act at school the way you act at home."

Jamaal does not know why he cannot learn like others. Is he not smart? Is he slow? But he realizes he cannot deal with the problem by acting up in class or Grandma will keep spanking him.

What will I do now? Jamaal thinks. *What can I do to make the other kids stop bothering me?*

Chapter 9

Picking Teams

Jamaal wants to play sports with his big brothers and their friends. But there's only one reason they ever invite him.

One summer morning, he and Keisha play with marbles in the living room when Darryl comes to the front door.

"Jamaal, come out and play with us!" he shouts.

When Jamaal gets outside, he realizes why he's being called out: they need a tenth player for basketball.

Jamaal is six years younger than Darryl—who they call D.J.—and he looks up to his oldest brother. D.J. excels in football and baseball, but he is a troublemaker at school. He also resists the authority of adults.

"Stop being so hard-headed," Mom always says to D.J.

In the basketball game, Jamaal guards D.J., who does not play too hard. Jamaal gets too aggressive with his defense. D.J., frustrated for a moment, lowers his shoulder, knocks his little brother down, and scores an easy layup.

D.J. walks back toward Jamaal and extends his hand to help his little brother up.

Jamaal sneers and refuses to accept the help.

"I'm going to be better than you," Jamaal says quietly.

D.J.'s eyes get big. He is stunned by his six-year-old brother's bold statement.

When the cousins play tag, Jamaal shines because he is so quick. But the older kids do not like to include Jamaal in baseball, basketball, or football games because he still whines and cries too much.

On any given day, the children count up who is available to play. Two designated captains select players for each team, and Jamaal is *always* the odd kid out.

"We don't want to play with you," one neighbor boy says as Jamaal cries. "You cry too much!"

Grandma hears the fuss, and comes outside.

"Y'all can't treat him that way," she says. "You better let him play and take turns or *nobody* is playing. I'll send everyone home!"

When Grandma goes back in the house, though, the kids just pick on Jamaal more for crying and getting them in trouble.

"You're such a crybaby, Ja-Millie," one cousin says to Jamaal. "And you are terrible at basketball. Leave us alone!"

They do not adjust the teams to include Jamaal.

He rushes back into the house to tell Grandma.

"They're still not letting me play," he reports to her, tears flowing down his face. "They say I'm no good at basketball."

GRANDMA'S RULE

"Don't let anybody tell you what you can and can't do," Grandma says, looking Jamaal squarely in the eyes. "God has given you the strength to do great things."

The two walk back outside.

"That's it!" she yells. "I warned y'all. This game is over. Everyone go home!"

Dotherightthingevenwhennoonei
lookingBelieveinyourselfandfoll
yourdreamsWithapositiveattitu
andhardworkyoucanachieveanyth

BekindtoyourclassmatesRespec
othersfeelingsHavefunbesillyan
laughReachforth   rs

Beanallstar.Do   rgettobeawes
S   itiveInspireyo
                        stthattheycan
                        ysdoyourbest

T
                  gnborhowyouwouldlike

Chapter 10

The Reading Test

At school, Jamaal excels at math. He likes numbers. He adds, subtracts, and multiples them with confidence. But two things terrify him: reading in general and, even worse, reading in front of others.

Sometimes teachers call upon students to read portions of a book out loud.

Jamaal badly wants to string the letters together so he can recognize them, read them, and understand them. But to him, they are a chaotic jumble of letters.

He squints his eyes to focus more, but he still cannot read the paragraph.

Four classmates snicker and laugh.

"He can't read," one whispers. "He doesn't even know how to pronounce any words!"

Jamaal wonders why he can't read like his classmates.

In that moment, he wishes he could disappear. But his only choice is to sink into his seat. He hopes the jokes end in class and do not follow him the entire day.

THE READING TEST

At Grandma's, ShanDerrick, who is often called Shan, tries to help Jamaal practice reading. But Shan loses patience with his little brother because it takes him too long to make any progress.

"Come on, Shan," Jamaal says. "I just want to go outside and play sports."

After a few weeks of third grade, Jamaal must take several reading tests. He is nervous.

Will they figure out what's wrong with me? Jamaal wonders. *Can the teachers help me?*

In one test, Jamaal looks at pictures and spells the object.

In a second test, Jamal pronounces the words and spells them.

Afterwards, he rushes to his mom.

"How did it go?" Mom asks.

Jamaal does not answer. His mind races, as a blur of words seem to surround him. He just wants to go home, far away from the confusing tests.

Chapter 11

Uncle Karl

Jamaal and his brothers know better than to disobey elders. No one instills more fear in kids than Uncle Karl.

Talk back to any adult, and Uncle Karl takes off his belt and spanks you. Forget to clean up a mess, and Uncle Karl takes off his belt and spanks you.

And he hardly talks.

More than anything, though, Uncle Karl pushes his nephews and cousins to take school seriously. Sometimes Jamaal's brothers stay at Uncle Karl's house before tests. Uncle Karl quizzes them on their words or facts. He spanks them if they do not focus or get too many answers wrong.

One day Kevin tries to cheat. He puts his spelling words on a piece of paper on the floor, underneath the dining room table. Without saying a word, Uncle Karl bends down, picks up the paper, yanks out his belt, lifts Kevin up out of his chair, and spanks him.

Hard.

Spanking is common in Port Arthur at the time, but is not as common today.

"Why is he so mean?" Kevin asks.

Darryl and Shan hear stories about Uncle Karl when he was younger.

Of his siblings, Karl was the smartest and fastest.

He starred in basketball. He was an exceptional shooter and ball handler, dribbling behind his back and through his legs, up and down the streets for hours at a time.

He showed potential in football.

He jumped 6 feet 2 inches in the high jump as a ninth grader.

The high jump mark was really special, but Karl's favorite sport was basketball.

Karl smoked a cigarette during a high school track meet, and his coach sent him home on a bus. The track coach also told Karl's basketball coach, even though basketball did not start for another month. The basketball coach told Karl he could not be on the team anymore.

Karl was heartbroken. *What will I do if I cannot play basketball?*

Karl lost the spirit to keep his grades up or pursue other sports and activities. He got into fights and skipped school. A counselor tried to help. The principal tried to help.

"You can go to college, especially for track," Principal Ross told Karl. "All you have to do is go to class and graduate from high school."

Karl was a great athlete and a smart student. But he was stubborn and dropped out of school in 11th grade.

He tried several different jobs and eventually settled on working in construction. Karl then started supporting himself and his family. Sometimes he wonders, *What if?*

Though he isn't much of a talker, Uncle Karl does make a point to tell his nephews, nieces, and younger cousins one message.

UNCLE KARL'S RULE

"Don't be like me," Uncle Karl says. "Don't quit school. It's not worth it—trust me."

Uncle Karl wants them to learn from his mistakes. If not, they will also pay a price.

Chapter 12

Rae-Rae Runs

All of Jamaal's cousins like to play sports, especially when the family hangs out. The kids join in for basketball, football, or relay races around Grandma's block—with the exception of Rae-Rae.

Rae-Rae does not like to do anything that gets her dirty. She is very particular about her hair and what she wears.

When Tae-Tae is the quarterback of the flag football team, Rae-Rae decides it would be fun to be a cheerleader.

Jamaal sees Tae-Tae and her sister Rae-Rae a lot. He enjoys being around them. To Jamaal, they seem to have the perfect family: Nanny Arlene and Uncle Robert own a house, eat dinner every day with their girls, and attend all their activities.

In middle school, Rae-Rae finds a sport she does love: track. She realizes her talent during P.E. class, when she has to take part in sports. She lines up for a race and, without really trying, wins!

Nanny Arlene and Uncle Robert are friends with the middle school track coach, Mr. Salisbury, who encourages Rae-Rae to join the team. But it is in high school under track coach Ora Smith that she excels even more.

Rae-Rae watches the 1996 Summer Olympics in Atlanta, and she lights up when she sees Gail Devers. She is the world's fastest woman, winning the gold medal in the 100-meter sprint, *and* she looks gorgeous! She competes with makeup, long fingernails, and accessories. Oh, and her smile. Gail's smile lights up the track!

Rae-Rae realizes she may get sweaty in track, but she will not get dirty. Plus, she can look as glamorous as she wants. That is just perfect for her!

Rae-Rae invites Jamaal to watch one of her track meets. Jamaal wants to get as close as possible, so he leans up against the fence and looks for his cousin. She participates in several events: the 100-meter hurdles, 300-meter hurdles, long jump, triple jump, and the 4 x 400 and 4 x 100 relays.

TRACK GLOSSARY

Hurdles: On a usual oval-shaped track, 100 meters is one of the long stretches. Competitors must jump over hurdles evenly spaced in front of them. The best in this event barely skim the top of each hurdle and run fast.

Long jump: The competitor begins with a sprint to build up speed then jumps when they reach the "takeoff" board. The winner leaps the farthest in the sand pit.

Triple jump: The competitor runs, reaches the "takeoff" board and leaps from one foot. The athlete then jumps from the other foot, and finally leaps again from the first foot, landing as far as possible in the sand pit.

Relays: Four-member teams run equal parts. So in the 4 x 400, everyone on the team must run 400 meters, which is one full lap around a typical track. In the 4 x 100, each athlete must run 100 meters. Each athlete hands a baton—usually a small aluminum stick—to the next athlete in pre-marked zones. The best relay teams are fast and smoothly pass the baton to one another.

There are hundreds of people in the stands. Jamaal feels the excitement in the air. Rae-Rae looks serious as she stretches and does some short jumps to warm up. Then she crouches down and places her left foot in the starting block—a piece of aluminum or metal that sprinters push off from.

The gun sounds. Rae-Rae runs hard and jumps over the first hurdle. She steps, explodes, and jumps over another hurdle. Then another. And another.

She is the first to cross the line. She raises her arms in victory, scans the crowd for her mom and dad, and smiles.

Jamaal falls in love with track!

Rae-Rae also wins the 300-meter hurdle, both relays, and both jumps. Afterward, she puts on a jacket and meets her family.

"Rae-Rae, you won everything!" Jamaal says excitedly. "Are you tired?"

Rae-Rae laughs and smiles. "I'm good. Thanks for coming, Jamaal! It's a lot of fun. You should try it!"

Maybe I will, Jamaal thinks.

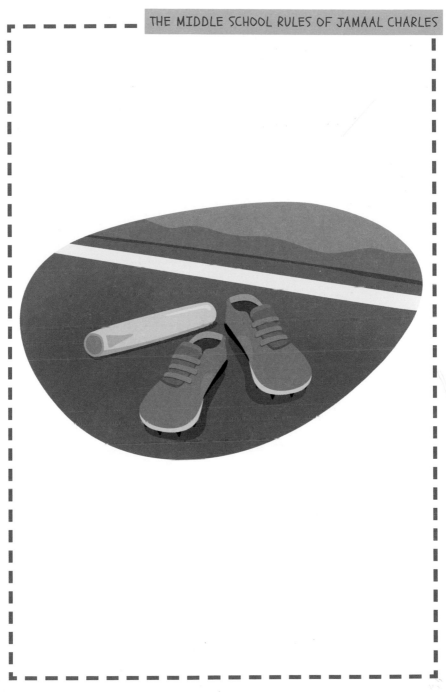

Chapter 13

Special Field Trip

As he suspected, Jamaal did not excel in the reading tests. He enters the special education program at Sam Houston Elementary School. Students in special education need extra help because of a medical, emotional, or learning challenge.

Jamaal does not mind the classroom, the teacher, or the other students. But he does mind that he does not get to go on field trips like some of his friends in other classes. His friend Randall rides the bus to the Fire Museum in nearby Beaumont and gets a red fire hat.

"No fair!" Jamaal says.

In the fourth grade, during the spring, Jamaal gets a surprise.

"Everyone, today we're going on a special field trip," Jamaal's teacher says. "Let's line up near the door, please."

"Where are we going?" one classmate whispers to Jamaal.

He shrugs.

They ride the bus for about 30 minutes, and Jamaal sees a sign for Beaumont.

Maybe we're going to the Fire Museum, Jamaal thinks.

The bus pulls into a school with a field and track. Hundreds of kids are there, along with dozens of adults.

Jamaal is happy to get off the bus; it does not have air conditioning and it is hot.

Jamaal and his classmates walk toward the grass inside the track. He notices other kids walk and talk in ways he has never seen before.

He does not pay attention as someone talks over the public address system. But something catches his interest.

"We are going to start with the 100-meter dash in a few minutes," the announcer says.

Jamaal wants to race!

An adult guides him toward the starting line. He takes his spot in a middle lane.

"Hi, my... name is... Andrew... and... I... am from... Stowell." The boy pauses and blinks a lot as he speaks.

"Hi, I'm Jamaal," Jamaal responds. "I'm from Port Arthur."

The announcer instructs the competitors to get ready. Then the gun sounds, and Jamaal takes off. He only looks straight ahead at the finish line. Jamaal wants to get there first!

Jamaal easily wins the 100-meter dash. He emphatically raises his arms as he crosses the finish line. His body feels alive!

And he wants to compete again.

Later, he wins the 200-meter and the long jump too. He can't wait to tell his mom, brothers, Grandma, and Rae-Rae. They'll all be so proud.

First he must collect the hardware!

Hours later, after all the events are over, there is a medal ceremony.

"Jamaal Charles, Sam Houston Elementary School in Port Arthur," the announcer says.

Jamaal's classmates and teachers clap and high-five. He walks toward the podium, which is an elevated platform. There are three tiers, and an adult leads him to the highest one!

Another adult smiles, shakes Jamaal's right hand, and places a gold-colored medal around his neck. Jamaal cannot go too far away. He has two more gold medals to receive!

On the bus ride back to school, everyone wants to touch and wear Jamaal's medals. His friends recount his great runs.

For once, Jamaal is the center of attention for a positive reason!

When he arrives at Grandma's, Jamaal runs into Kevin on the front porch.

"How did you get all those medals?" Kevin asks.

Jamaal does not answer. He races toward his mom.

"Look at all these awards I won!" Jamaal says.

"You won all *that*?" she exclaims.

Mom, Grandma, Kevin, and Shan listen as Jamaal shares about his special field trip.

Mom explains what the event was all about.

It was organized by the Special Olympics—the world's largest sports organization for children and adults with intellectual disabilities. That describes a person who learns and develops more slowly than others.

Grandma opens up the encyclopedia and finds more information: Special Olympics provides millions of athletes from hundreds of countries the chance to strive, compete, and dream.

"It was the best day ever!" Jamaal says. "I want to sign up for the Port Arthur Flyers!"

Nanny Arlene, Uncle Robert, and other community leaders founded the Flyers and many of the Killer Millers joined the team.

Chapter 14

Mourning Grandma

Weeks later, Jamaal walks toward Grandma's house. He notices a lot of cars in the street and relatives on the front porch.

Upon reaching the porch, Jamaal sees aunties, uncles, and cousins quiet and sad. Most of them have swollen eyes, like they have been crying.

"What's going on?" Jamaal asks.

"Grandma died," one cousin says.

Jamaal runs to a bedroom, crying.

No, no, no, he weeps. *She didn't die. She can't die. She's the only one who understands me.*

So many thoughts and questions race through Jamaal's mind. He thought people lived forever. He thought Grandma would *always* be there for him.

No one close to him has ever died. *How could it be Grandma? Where did she go? What did I do? What do I do now?*

Jamaal cries and cries. Kevin finds Jamaal, and they cry together. Though three years older, Kevin does not understand death either. The only thing that makes them briefly feel better is punching and kicking the wall. But afterwards, all that's left are holes and sore hands and feet.

That night, Jamaal cannot sleep. He sits on the porch with his family.

The sky is dark and clear under the glow of a full moon. But near midnight, they cannot believe their eyes.

A halo of light radiates above Grandma's house.

"Look at that," D.J. says. "It's like someone switched on a light."

"I've never seen anything so beautiful," one auntie says. "Praise God for a sign from heaven."

Days later, Jamaal prepares for his first funeral. They cannot

hold the service at Zion Hill because it is just too small. The family expects over 1,000 people to pay their respect to Grandma.

At the front of the big church lies a box. Jamaal learns Grandma is in there. But he is too afraid to look inside the box. He does not want to see her this way.

Grandma once said she did not want a big funeral. But she does not have a choice; thousands are inside the church. During the service, many people line up to share stories about her. They are not surprising: Grandma said or did something kind.

She was extraordinary in her simplicity. One life, a hundred stories, all saying the same thing.

People tell stories of home-cooked meals delivered to

hurting friends, cash given to help pay a bill, a phone call offering encouragement and support.

As the service winds down, Jamaal still does not understand death. But the stories and memories of his Grandma stay with him forever. He knows that many people loved his Grandma, and he believes she is in heaven with God.

Chapter 15

Ducking and Dodging

At Sam Houston Elementary School, the principal's office is on the right. Keep going straight, and there is a long hallway. Most of the classrooms are in other parts of the school, but the two for Special Ed are among the few in that hallway. Jamaal is ashamed to be in Special Ed. He tries to hide that information from his friends and teammates.

What will they think of me? he wonders. *Will they laugh at me?*

Between classes, Jamaal often waits until the bell rings. When most students are in their classroom, Jamaal stealthily moves through the hallways and slips into Special Ed.

But other kids figure out Jamaal's secret.

"Why are you going in there?" Jimmy asks Jamaal. "That's the class for dummies."

Jimmy and two other boys laugh out loud.

Jamaal does not say a word. He is not good at coming up with funny or mean comebacks. Instead, he hurries into class and sinks into his seat.

Jamaal does not act up in class much anymore, and he focuses on becoming a better reader. One afternoon, Jamaal hears his name over the intercom.

"Jamaal Charles, please come to the principal's office."

"Ooohhh," classmates say at the same time.

Jamaal panics.

Did someone in my family get hurt? he wonders.

When he arrives in Principal Remington's office, Jamaal sits in a big leather chair. A shiny wooden desk is between him and Principal Remington.

"What's wrong, Principal Remington?" Jamaal asks. "Is everyone in my family OK?"

"Well, Mrs. Conway says you stole $20 out of her purse during lunch," Principal Remington says.

Jamaal looks confused.

"No I didn't," Jamaal says.

During lunch, Mrs. Conway says Jamaal spent $4 on lunch and several snacks, including a candy bar.

"Where did you get the money?" Principal Remington asks.

"I got it from my big brother Shan," Jamaal says.

"Mrs. Conway says you climbed the outside wall to her window on the second level and stole that money from her purse," Principal Remington says. "You are suspended from school for three days for stealing."

Jamaal starts to cry.

When his mom arrives to pick him up, Jamaal struggles to speak because he is so upset.

"Mom," Jamaal says with tears in his eyes, "I promise I didn't do it."

The next day, right before school starts, Mom demands to speak to Principal Remington. Though he is busy, he recognizes the very serious look on her face.

They enter his office. Principal Remington closes the door.

"This is ridiculous," Mom says. "My boys do not steal. I leave money around all the time. They know not to touch what does not belong to them."

MOM'S RULE

"I teach my kids, 'If it's not yours, don't take it. If you need it, ask for it.'"

Mom insists that Principal Remington investigate the matter further.

He agrees.

"I'll follow up tomorrow," he says.

"No, you address this now," Mom says. "Jamaal and I will wait right here."

Principal Remington heads upstairs and visits Mrs. Conway's classroom. She does not have any students at the time. He asks her to retrace her actions the previous morning and check any jacket pockets or drawers.

Mrs. Conway reflects for a moment.

She walks to her desk at the front of the classroom, and pulls open the main drawer.

She turns red.

"There's the $20 bill," she says sheepishly.

"How do you know that's it?" Principal Remington asks.

"Because there's a small blue mark on the top corner," Mrs. Conway says.

The two of them return to Principal Remington's office.

"I'm so embarrassed and sorry," Mrs. Conway says to Jamaal. "I found the money. It was wrong of me to accuse you of taking it. I hope you can forgive me."

Jamaal's mom is furious. Her son already has a hard enough time in school. *Now this?* But she and Jamaal take deep breaths and decide to forgive Mrs. Conway.

Chapter 16

Chicken Runs for Paw Paw

Jamaal really misses his Grandma. Things are not the same without her: No Sunday dinner, no regular church attendance from most family members, and no anchor to count on.

Everyone hurts, but no one more than Paw Paw. He does not laugh as much. He's not as active. And he's not as healthy; he spends most of his time lying in bed.

The person who is at the house most is Jamaal, and Paw Paw sends him on special missions.

"Here's $5," Paw Paw tells Jamaal. "Go to Church's Chicken and get me a two-piece meal with mashed potatoes and strawberry lemonade."

Jamaal does as his Paw Paw says; he sprints the three blocks to Church's, orders the food, then sprints back to the house, the bag of food in one hand, the drink in the other.

Sometimes Jamaal hears the neighborhood dogs

79

barking, which scares him. That makes him run even faster.

Jamaal runs to Paw Paw's bedroom, and hands him the bag of food, the drink and, usually, change. $1.50 to be precise; Paw Paw's meal costs $3.50. Jamaal sometimes buys fries or a pop for himself. Because he has a big appetite, though, Jamaal cannot afford to buy an entire meal.

Like Grandma, Paw Paw looks after Jamaal. In the winter, a teacher calls Paw Paw at the house because Jamaal talks and acts up in class.

"Do you have a belt?" Paw Paw asks the teacher. "I just want you to know you can spank him." Paw Paw asks the teacher to hand the phone to Jamaal.

"If she has to call me one more time," Paw Paw says, "she's going to spank you, then it's going to be between you and me when you get home."

That means double the trouble!

Jamaal hands the phone back to his teacher, returns to his seat, and does not say another word for the remainder of the day or week.

Like Grandma, Paw Paw also defends Jamaal.

Jamaal loves sports, though he is not a natural star like others in the family. Many believe Shan could be the best running back in the area since Joe Washington—a Pro Bowl and Super Bowl running back in the NFL! His cousin Terry is nicknamed Bo, as in Bo Jackson—an All-Star in professional baseball *and* football. And Tae-Tae and Rae-Rae dominate their respective sports and already draw interest from major colleges.

Jamaal, meanwhile, struggles in track because he is not very fast. In Texas, the most popular track event is the 100-meter sprint and the 4 x 100-meter relay. The winner of the 100-meter final at the Olympics earns two titles: champion and world's fastest man.

In elementary school, Jamaal joins the Port Arthur Flyers and competes in three events. He tries the hurdles, which no one else in his age division does. Consistently jumping over the hurdles is a problem for Jamaal.

"Ouch," one track teammate says, as he watches Jamaal trip on a hurdle in practice. "You are so clumsy. Can you not fall? It hurts just watching you. Maybe hurdles aren't for you, man."

Jamaal ignores him, wincing as he tends to scratches on his knees from the fall. Minutes later, he returns to the starting block and tries again. He clears four hurdles but clips the fifth and tumbles again.

Some teammates say he should quit.

Jamaal refuses.

PAW PAW'S RULE

"Don't you listen to other people," Paw Paw tells Jamaal. "You've got everything you need to be successful."

Chapter 17

Ms. Conner

Jamaal does not like Special Ed. There are 30 students... and one teacher. He feels the teacher does not take enough time to help *him*.

At Woodrow Wilson Middle School, however, his experience changes. His Special Ed classes only have 15 students and there are multiple teachers to work with. There are also teacher aides who can help.

Ms. Conner is Jamaal's teacher for math and English. She knows that he loves sports, and she hears he is a good teammate. That means Jamaal knows how to work well with others.

Ms. Conner notices that Jamaal does not raise his hand to answer questions and does not ever ask for help. She decides Jamaal needs one-on-one attention.

"How are you today?" Ms. Conner says, as she pulls a desk next to Jamaal's in the back of the classroom.

Jamaal wonders if he has done something wrong.

"Uh, I'm fine, Ms. Conner," Jamaal says. "How are you?"

"Thank you for asking, Jamaal," she responds. "I am doing very well. I'm excited to spend some time with you working on your words."

Jamaal quietly reads to Ms. Conner, and they discuss the

words and stories. When the bell rings, Jamaal cannot believe it: 30 minutes pass so quickly!

He feels good.

"Jamaal, remember this," Ms. Conner says as she stands up. "Every student in this school faces challenges, not just in this classroom."

Jamaal's class disrupts Ms. Conner a lot, and they misbehave sometimes. But Jamaal likes that Ms. Conner never gets upset and never sends anyone to the principal's office.

Ms. Conner is patient and positive. If Jamaal does not comprehend something at first, Ms. Conner figures out another approach. When Jamaal gets angry that he cannot read a particular word or sentence, Ms. Conner tells him to take a deep breath and try again.

Jamaal is not afraid to ask Ms. Conner for help now. He trusts her.

As the school year progresses, Ms. Conner senses something

about Jamaal: he embraces a challenge. Deep down, Jamaal is a competitor, driven to succeed, not just in sports. But she wants Jamaal to remember something.

MS. CONNER'S RULE

"Be patient with yourself," Ms. Conner tells Jamaal. "Don't be so hard on yourself."

Sixth grade is the best year Jamaal has ever had in school. Fortunately for Jamaal, he'll have Ms. Conner in seventh and eighth grade too!

Chapter 18

Classroom Courtroom

Ms. Conner is not the only teacher Jamaal really likes at school. Miss Hamilton teaches social studies, which explores history and geography, among other topics.

Jamaal and his classmates just cannot dislike the class—Miss Hamilton loves teaching so much.

Miss Hamilton also knows Jamaal's family: she ran track in high school with his mom. They were even on a relay team together!

Miss Hamilton is creative, and she can be silly, sometimes wearing a costume from whatever period of time they are studying.

She has a saying: "I am here because I want to be. You are here because you have to be. But together, we can make each other be the best we can be."

Near Miss Hamilton's desk is a picture board that reads, "Me, You, Us."

"Whatever makes you happy," she tells the students, "bring it. Pictures, quotes, whatever."

As a Special Ed teacher, Miss Hamilton brings the lessons to life. She invites students to reenact historic scenes, and then they discuss them afterward.

Miss Hamilton recognizes a style of teaching that works especially well with Jamaal. When it is time to take a test, Miss Hamilton reads the questions to Jamaal, and he tells her the answers.

Jamaal's grades improve!

As they learn about the wild, wild West, Jamaal makes a panorama box—a broad view of a particular image—that features cowboys made out of toothpicks.

In class, though, Jamaal still does not like to talk in front of others or answer questions out loud. One of Miss Hamilton's activities draws him out.

If someone does something wrong, Miss Hamilton turns the classroom into a courtroom. She puts on a black robe, grabs her gavel—a piece of wood that sort of looks like a hammer—and sits behind her desk.

Miss Hamilton keeps her classroom very clean, and she does not have many rules. One of them, however, is not to chew gum.

When they walk into class one day, Judge Hamilton, sitting at her bench, slams the gavel down and says, "Order in the court!"

She calls Tom to stand before her.

"Please walk to your desk and look underneath it," Judge Hamilton says.

Tom slowly walks toward the door and turns to his right. He peaks underneath his desk.

"What do you see?" Judge Hamilton asks.

"I see a piece of gum," Tom slowly says.

"Who does it belong to?" Judge Hamilton asks.

"Not me!" Tom says.

"I see," Judge Hamilton says. "Remain there, Tom."

Judge Hamilton calls Jackson before her. Jackson is Tom's best friend.

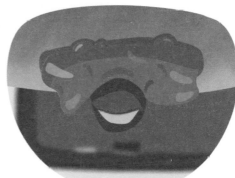

"Do you swear to tell the truth, the whole truth, and nothing but the truth?"

"I do," Jackson says.

"Jackson, have you ever seen Tom chew gum?"

"Yes, ma'am."

"Does he chew gum a lot?"

"Yes, ma'am."

"Do you know what *kind* of gum he likes to chew?"

"I've only ever seen him chew Big Red," Jackson replies.

"Oh, yes, the cinnamon flavored gum. Tom, please grab a tissue and remove the piece of gum from under your desk."

Tom sighs and follows the judge's orders.

"Now, take that gum to Jackson," Judge Hamilton demands.

Tom walks over to Jackson.

"What does that smell like, Jackson?"

"Umm..." Jackson stammers.

"Remember the oath you took to tell the truth." Judge Hamilton reminds him.

"Cinnamon," Jackson responds.

"Do you know anyone other than Tom who chews Big Red in this class?"

"No, ma'am."

"Thank you for your cooperation."

Judge Hamilton asks Tom to stand before her again.

"Let me ask you again, Tom, who does that piece of gum belong to?"

Tom does not immediately answer.

Jamaal chimes in.

"Oh, you're storying," he says. "You know you did it. Don't lie. Tell the truth."

Miss Hamilton always appreciates Jamaal's honesty. It's a quality in him that she admires.

"OK," Tom quietly says. "I did it. That was my gum."

Everyone claps.

Judge Hamilton taps her gavel.

"Order in the court! Order in the court!"

Judge Hamilton's eyes soften.

"Let this be something you all live by," she says.

JUDGE HAMILTON'S RULE

"Tell the truth," she says, "and be accountable for your actions."

Judge Hamilton sentences Tom to clean up the classroom after school for the remainder of the week. Miss Hamilton is proud that Jamaal had the courage to speak up in class, even though his comment was, technically, out of order!

The proceeding reinforces to Jamaal the importance of being accountable for your actions.

As their relationship grows, Miss Hamilton gives Jamaal more and more responsibility. She sends him to her car to grab a box she forgot, or to deliver the attendance slips to the office.

She appreciates that Jamaal is humble, dependable, and trustworthy.

Jamaal appreciates that Miss Hamilton believes in him.

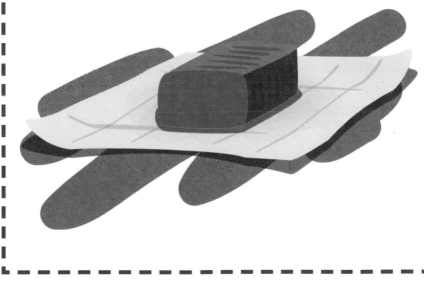

Chapter 19

Always Be Respectful

Jamaal feels most comfortable playing sports. On a field, a court or a track, actions speak louder than words.

In the locker room or on the bus, Jamaal rarely says anything. Teammates discuss their practices or games. They hype up the latest songs or movies and debate which college football teams are best. Jamaal may be around the conversation, but he's never in it. Though he does not isolate himself, he also does not offer many observations or opinions.

In middle school, Jamaal is closest to his brother Kevin.

They fuss at one another, and they still argue over video games, but Kevin does not make fun of Jamaal anymore and he watches out for his little brother.

Kevin's personality is very different from Jamaal's. He is mostly happy, a jokester who is also very spontaneous. That means he often does things that are not planned, and he follows ideas that pop into his head.

Kevin is always on the go: to the swimming pool, to the park to play football, to a friend's to play video games. Jamaal always tags along. He likes to spend time with his brother.

In seventh grade, during a Special Ed class, Jamaal makes fun of a female classmate because of the size of her feet.

"I saw a clown in the hallway," Jamaal says, "and he wants his shoes back."

Classmates laugh.

"Don't make fun of me," Belinda firmly says.

"Seriously, though, is Tim Duncan of the Spurs your brother?" Jamaal asks.

"No," Belinda replies, "but Jack is— and he's going beat you up!"

Jamaal keeps laughing.

"Well," he says, "go get your big brother. I've got three big brothers!"

After class, another classmate approaches Jamaal.

"You know Belinda is serious," he says. "Her brother Jack is a football player *and* an eighth grader. You better watch out!"

When school ends that day, Jamaal hears that Jack is on the hunt for him. Jamaal sneaks out a side door, behind a teacher, and he runs home.

"Kevin, Kevin, Kevin!" Jamaal yells.

Kevin is on the phone.

"What's all that noise?" Kevin asks. "Man, I'm talking to somebody. Leave me alone."

Jamaal waits, and he waits. Thirty minutes pass. As soon as Kevin hangs up, Jamaal is there to tell him what happened.

"I got this," Kevin says.

Jamaal feels like he can finally exhale. He trusts Kevin.

The next morning, Jamaal and Kevin walk toward school. They

see Jack waiting near the main entrance.

"I need to speak to you, Jamaal," Jack says, slamming his right fist into his left hand. "I hear you're bothering my little sister."

Jack approaches Jamaal, but Kevin steps in front of him.

"I'm Jamaal's big brother, and I got a message for you," Kevin says confidently. "Don't put your hand on him, or there will be serious consequences."

With his eyes big, Jamaal awaits Jack's response. Jack unfurls his fist.

"Tell him to leave my sister alone then!" Jack says.

Kevin nods and glances over at Jamaal.

"I'm sorry," Jamaal says quietly, looking toward Belinda. Belinda rolls her eyes while Jack turns to head into school.

The handful of students who crowded around also walk toward the front entrance.

KEVIN'S RULE

"Be respectful of other people," Kevin tells Jamaal. "I'm not always going to be here to protect you."

Respect is a word Grandma always talked about. But maybe, Jamaal thinks, he has forgotten about her rules for a while. He will not soon forget to respect others after the incident with Belinda and Jack!

"Thanks, Kevin," Jamaal says.

"No problem, little bro."

Chapter 20

Beating Danny

At Woodrow Wilson Middle School, they hand out awards at the end of the school year. Several relatives win Athlete of the Year, including D.J., Shan, Tae-Tae, and Rae-Rae.

Jamaal wants to be next.

"I want to win Athlete of the Year," Jamaal tells Kevin.

In seventh grade, Jamaal is not the athlete he wants to be. He has a solid football season, mostly as a cornerback. But he puts in extra work, focusing on his strength and speed.

By the spring Jamaal thinks he might even have a shot at the 4x100 relay team!

One day Jamaal comes to school and sees everyone crowded around somebody. He gets closer and then realizes who it is: Danny Gorrer.

Jamaal had played sports against Danny as a kid; Danny was a good athlete. After spending two years in North Carolina, Danny has moved back to Port Arthur—and he's a *great* athlete now.

At the first summer track practice, Danny beats everyone in the 100-meter dash by a big margin. Coach makes the boys run it again. Danny runs even faster. Jamaal finishes fifth.

Uh-oh, he thinks.

Jamaal does not make the relay team. But he still has the hurdles.

He practices over and over, although he does not complete many of the early-season races because of falls. Each time he falls Jamaal dusts himself off and waits for the next practice or meet.

Jamaal does not win any hurdle races, but he qualifies for

the regional meet in Houston. If he finishes first or second in either the 110- or 300-meter hurdles (or both), Jamaal will head to the Junior Olympics in Buffalo, New York.

Jamaal places fourth in the 300-meter hurdle race; he clips two hurdles, slowing him down, but he crosses the finish line.

He then sets his sights on the 110-meter hurdle race. It is the final event of the meet.

Jamaal easily qualifies for the final. He believes he can win the title *and go* to the Junior Olympics.

When the gun sounds for the final, Jamaal explodes out of the block, and smoothly clears the first two hurdles. He is leading the race!

"Maybe Jamaal has finally figured this out!" a teammate says.

Jamaal clears the next three hurdles without any issue. He widens his lead.

He approaches the sixth hurdle, and he launches skyward. But his lead foot—actually his big toe—bumps the top of the hurdle.

Jamaal's body hurtles forward. His right leg also crashes into the hurdle. The hurdle falls over and then on top of him. In a split second, every other competitor blows by him. Jamaal is not in the top two. Jamaal does not even finish the race.

Tears stream down his face. He is not physically hurt; he's just very, very disappointed. Another fall, another fail.

Should I keep doing the hurdles? he wonders.

After an intense summer of working out every day, Jamaal wants to be the starting running back, just like his big brother. Shan is in high school now, and he dominates. Colleges from far and wide come to his games and offer him athletic scholarships.

Jamaal shines in training camp, making defenders miss left and right. His teammates notice that he has improved a lot. Danny does not have Jamaal's moves, but Danny has flat-out speed.

The coaches *love* speed and make Danny the starting running back.

Still wanting to win Athlete of the Year, Jamaal comes up with an idea: he'll play *more* sports! Danny, after all, only runs track and plays football.

RB DEPTH CHART

1. Danny Gorrer
2. Jamaal Charles

In addition to football, basketball, and track, Jamaal signs up for tennis and golf. But at the end of the school year, Danny wins the award for Male Athlete of the Year.

"Don't give up, Jamaal," Shan tells Jamaal. "Keep working hard. It'll pay off."

Next year, Jamaal thinks. *There's always next year.*

Jamaal sometimes wonders why his life seems so hard. But he refuses to give up on himself.

Chapter 21
The Shan Dive

Jamaal dreams of becoming a football star, but he already lives with one. Shan paves the path in the classroom and on the field. Shan is an excellent student, earning all A's.

Shan knows that Jamaal sees him as a role model, so he comes to Woodrow Wilson Middle School sometimes to pick Jamaal up. That's a big deal because everyone—students and teachers—know who ShanDerrick Charles is.

Mr. Williams, the head coach of Lincoln High School in Port Arthur, even lets Jamaal hang around the football team. Jamaal is the only middle schooler Mr. Williams allows to watch games from the team's sideline and ride on the bus with the players!

Shan has a signature move when he scores a touchdown. He leaps across the goal line, with the ball stretched out. People call it the "Shan Dive."

He does it *all* the time. Then after he scores, Shan hands the ball to Jamaal. After games, Shan lets Jamaal carry his helmet and shoulder pads. Thousands of kids in Port Arthur would welcome that privilege.

Shan is always proud, kind, and respectful.

SHAN'S RULE
"Rep your family right," Shan tells Jamaal.

Another player is always around Shan. His name is Cal, and he is a freshman when Shan is a senior. They met the previous year, when Cal was invited by coaches to work out with the varsity players. That's a big deal.

Some of the older players wonder why Cal is there, but he quickly shows them: Cal can bench press a lot and squat 315 pounds. Because Cal is a freshman, the varsity football players do not like him at their parties or when he joins them for fast-food dinners. But who was going to tell Shan who he could and could not hang out with?

Cal closely watches how Shan studies, speaks to college recruiters, and interacts with fans both young and old.

As an act of gratitude to Shan, Cal decides he will mentor Jamaal. He buys Jamaal pizza from Little Caesar's, gives him clothes, and invites him to play video games at his dad's house. Then, they show up for the first time, on the same day, to the same church—Rock Island Baptist Church.

And they keep coming back. They love the energy and passion of the church members. As Jamaal and Cal grow closer, they pray together at church and sometimes in the car afterwards.

"God, lighten our load," they pray. "Make us better people, and put us in a better situation for life. Amen."

Jamaal is thankful that he's got his family, but he's also thankful that he has a new friend.

Chapter 22

Support Network

Jamaal feels safest at Grandma and Paw Paw's house. Everything is so familiar to him. But Jamaal lacks a routine, and Paw Paw's health declines so he spends more and more time in bed. For Jamaal, meals are unhealthy and inconsistent, bed time is up to him—which means lots of late nights—and free time is filled with too many video games and not enough books.

Jamaal asks his mom if he can move in with one of his youth basketball coaches: Kenneth Lofton. Paw Paw and Coach Lofton's father worked together at the shipyard. Also, Jamaal's mom babysat Coach Lofton when he was a boy.

Jamaal looks up to Coach Lofton and his wife Gina, who is an elementary school teacher. The Loftons also have a son named Geremiah who looks up to Jamaal.

Mrs. Lofton is from Louisiana, and she is an excellent cook. Jamaal's favorite dish Mrs. Lofton makes is jambalaya, a dish consisting of seasoned rice, vegetables, and chicken or sausage.

Geremiah has trouble reading and comprehending, much like Jamaal.

Mrs. Lofton sits Jamaal and Geremiah in front of the computer in the living room. They use educational websites to help them practice saying the words, working them into sentences and then into paragraphs.

They *love* the games and challenges!

Mrs. Lofton also brings plenty of books and resources from school, since she is a teacher.

Often among the youngest, Jamaal enjoys being a big brother to Geremiah. And Geremiah watches how hard Jamaal works in sports and with his studies.

Jamaal also learns a lot from Coach Lofton. His basketball team is called the Port Arthur H.E.A.T., which stands for Helping Educate Athletes Together, and he mentors many boys in town.

Coach Lofton is a respected man in the community, and he imparts an important message to the young men in his life.

COACH LOFTON'S RULE
"Always be humble and help others."

Jamaal also helps his coach.

One Sunday morning, Jamaal knocks on Coach Lofton's bedroom door.

"Are we going to church?" Jamaal asks.

"No, Jamaal," Coach Lofton says. "My favorite team, the Minnesota Vikings, are playing on TV."

Jamaal frowns.

"No, sir," Jamaal says. "We *need* to go to church. I've got to get my blessings!"

"Well," Coach Lofton says, "I guess we're going to church!"

Jamaal lives with Coach Lofton's family for about a year. But Jamaal mostly lives with his Nanny Arlene and Uncle Robert. They have lots of rules.

LEBLANC HOUSE RULES

God is the head of this household.
Education comes first, sports second.
Respect yourself, and respect others.
Keep your room clean.
Care for your cousins.
Finish what you start.

Uncle Robert would often say, "You can't do nothing 'til you do right!" In other words: kids do not get to make decisions until they abide by house rules.

But the change is difficult for Jamaal. He cries himself to sleep at night and asks, *Why me? Where is my Grandma? Where is my mom? Where is my dad?*

Jamaal's father is a topic not often discussed. Uncle Robert tries to provide perspective and encourage Jamaal.

"Your dad made a decision, and we're going to go on with life," Uncle Robert tells Jamaal. "Be better. Regardless of your situation, be a better person because God has given you the strength to handle a lot of things."

Jamaal wishes he did not have to take on so much. When is enough *enough?*

As weeks pass, Jamaal comes to appreciate his new home. He likes being around his cousin Tae-Tae, who is like a sister. He likes that Uncle Robert and Nanny Arlene drive him to practices, and he loves that they attend all of his games. He likes breakfast in the morning, and he loves family dinners most nights—unless there's a game—around the dining room table.

Jamaal also discovers that he likes structure. Immediately after school, before any sport or horseplay, the kids must do their homework in the kitchen.

No exceptions.

Uncle Robert and Nanny Arlene are kind and fun. But they are also strict about their rules. Uncle Robert tells Jamaal a story that happened years earlier, when Shan was living in their house.

FLASHBACK

AFTER SHAN GOT HIS DRIVER'S LICENSE, HE SOMETIMES SNUCK OUT AFTER EVERYONE WENT TO BED. HE WOULD PUSH HIS AUNT'S LEXUS SEDAN OUT OF THE GARAGE AND DRIVE TO VISIT FRIENDS.

ONE MORNING, HIS AUNT WALKED TO HER CAR TO DRIVE TO WORK AT THE OIL REFINERY. BUT SHE FELT HEAT COMING FROM THE HOOD OF HER CAR.

"OH," SHE SAID TO HERSELF, AS SHE PLACED HER RIGHT HAND ON THE CAR. "WHAT IS GOING ON?"

SHE CAME BACK INSIDE THE HOUSE.

"MY CAR IS WARM," SHE SAID. "SOMEONE WANT TO TELL ME WHY?"

SHANDERRICK LOWERED HIS HEAD.

"MA'AM, I TOOK THE CAR OUT TO VISIT ERIC WITHOUT YOUR PERMISSION," SHAN ADMITTED. "I'VE DONE IT SEVERAL TIMES LATELY."

THEY APPRECIATED THAT SHAN TOLD THEM THE TRUTH. BUT WHAT HE DID WAS DANGEROUS, WITH THE POSSIBILITY OF GETTING INTO AN ACCIDENT OR BEING ARRESTED. SUCH A GRAVE OFFENSE COULD NOT GO UNPUNISHED: SHAN COULD GO NOWHERE FOR TWO WEEKS.

Uncle Robert wraps up the story and tells Jamaal about an important rule.

UNCLE ROBERT'S RULE

"Trouble is easy to get into," Uncle Robert says, "and hard to get out of."

Chapter 23

Tithing

Other than Church's Chicken runs for Paw Paw, Jamaal does not get to handle money. In fact, money seems to be a constant problem in his family. That is why he never has any.

The kids get an allowance at Nanny Arlene and Uncle Robert's house. Each week, the kids must do chores, like taking out the trash, setting the table, folding clothes, etc. to receive cash—$10 each.

Rae-Rae likes to spend her money right away to buy fashion accessories and yummy snacks, and Tae-Tae likes to save her money and buy more expensive items like shoes. Jamaal hides his cash in a small box in his closet.

One Friday, after giving him a $10 bill, Uncle Robert invites Jamaal to sit at the dining room table.

"So Jamaal, what are you going to do with your money?" Uncle Robert asks.

Jamaal has no idea. Money is new to him! Will he buy the latest Michael Jordan sneakers? Or a new football? Maybe a real football jersey?

Uncle Robert sees Jamaal's focus drifting.

"Jamaal, let me tell you a story," he says.

FLASHBACK

WHEN UNCLE ROBERT AND NANNY ARLENE FIRST GOT MARRIED, THEY DID NOT MAKE VERY MUCH MONEY, AND THEY DID NOT HAVE ANY MONEY SAVED UP IN THE BANK. BUT GRANDMA SAID: "YOU MUST TITHE TO THE CHURCH."

TITHING IS A WAY TO HONOR GOD AND HELP GOD'S PEOPLE. A BELIEVER IS TO GIVE A PORTION OF THE MONEY HE OR SHE EARNS TO THE CHURCH TO SUPPORT PASTORS AND PEOPLE IN NEED, LIKE ORPHANS AND THE HOMELESS.

THAT DAY, GRANDMA TOLD A STORY FROM THE BIBLE. SHE EXPLAINED THAT TWO MEN NAMED ABRAHAM AND JACOB OFFERED TITHES TO THE LORD. THEN TITHING BECAME THE LAW IN ISRAEL.

WELL, NANNY ARLENE AND UNCLE ROBERT WRESTLED WITH THE IDEA OF TITHING. THEY WERE BEHIND ON PAYING THE RENT AND THE ELECTRICITY BILL. THEN, THEIR CAR BROKE DOWN.

BUT THEY PRAYED FOR GOD'S GRACE, AND THEY MADE A COMMITMENT TO KEEP ON TITHING NO MATTER WHAT.

"Do you know what happened, Jamaal?" Uncle Robert asks.

"No, sir," Jamaal responds.

"God started to open doors, and he put us in better situations," Uncle Robert says. "Over time, we got better jobs, two cars, and this house. All the while, we tithed and believed in God."

UNCLE ROBERT'S RULE

"If you give nothing to God," Uncle Robert says, "how do you expect God to give something back to you?"

Uncle Robert explains that the decision must be Jamaal's alone. He points to Malachi 3:10 in the Bible.

"'Bring the whole tithe into the storehouse, that there may be

THE MIDDLE SCHOOL RULES OF JAMAAL CHARLES

food in my house. Test me in this,' says the Lord Almighty, 'and see if I will not throw open the floodgates of heaven and pour out so much blessing that there will not be room enough to store it.'"

Two days later, on Sunday morning, Jamaal hands Nanny Arlene a $10 bill.

"Can you give me change for this?" Jamaal asks.

"What for?" Nanny Arlene says.

"I want to tithe at church today."

Nanny Arlene smiles and hugs Jamaal.

"I am so proud of you," she says.

Jamaal cannot wait to get to church!

During the church service, ushers come around the church and send a basket through each aisle. When the basket arrives, Jamaal fishes the $1 bill out of his pocket and proudly places it in the basket. He catches a peek of what's inside: checks, 5s, 20s, and even 100s!

He hopes all that money pleases God.

Chapter 24 Freshman Football

Shan gets several scholarship offers to play football. Colleges charge students money to take classes and earn degrees. Some students do not have to pay if the school offers them an academic or athletic scholarship. Shan accepts a full athletic scholarship at Southern Methodist University in Dallas.

He falls short of a few goals his senior year at Lincoln High School: he finishes 30 yards short of Joe Washington's career rushing record. He does not win the Willie Ray Smith Award, either, which is given to the best offensive player in southeast Texas.

Jamaal does not know what that award really is but it sounds like a big deal.

As a ninth grader, Jamaal starts at running back on the freshman team. Danny starts at quarterback. Danny gets moved up to junior varsity early in the season. That is one step away from the varsity team—the team thousands of fans pack the stadium to watch!

Jamaal welcomes the starting position on the freshman team. He believes his hard work in the summer will pay off, and he displays his conditioning during practices. Often, when he gets the ball as a running back, he runs full-speed into the end zone. Jamaal does that even if the play is whistled after just a few yards.

He leads the freshman team to a 7–2 record.

Danny, meanwhile, gets promoted again. He goes from junior varsity to the varsity team because his older brother Corey suffers a serious shoulder injury. Danny is one of just three freshmen in school history to start on varsity.

And Danny will start in a playoff game!

Jamaal also earns a promotion: he will be a reserve defensive back.

"I wish I could start at running back in that game," Jamaal says to Cal.

In practices against the starting varsity defense, Jamaal gets to play running back. He shows just how far he has come.

One of Lincoln's star players is a linebacker nicknamed Bae-Bae. He is big (5 feet 11 inches and 230 pounds), fast, and very physical. Jamaal lines up with the third-string offense—they are the *backups* to the backups.

The play call is a draw, which means the offense acts like they are going to pass the ball. The quarterback waits, then gives a delayed handoff to the running back.

Jamaal gets the ball. He sprints straight up the middle of the field, approaching Bae-Bae. Jamaal fakes left, fakes right, then he explodes back to the left.

Bae-Bae is left flat-footed.

"Ooohh-eee," a senior offensive starter says.

The next play, Jamaal gets the ball, and he blows past Bae-Bae again.

Still, the coaches will not let Jamaal play running back in the playoffs. In a game that Lincoln is winning big, he does get to enter the game in the final minutes as a cornerback.

Here's my chance, Jamaal thinks. *I'll show them I belong on varsity.*

On the second play, the opposing quarterback throws a ball toward him, and Jamaal mistimes his jump. The receiver hauls the ball in and runs the final 25 yards into the end zone for a touchdown.

Jamaal is one and done. He does not play another varsity snap as a freshman. He'll have to wait until next year.

Another setback? Jamaal starts to see them differently now. The embarrassments and disappointments used to discourage him. Now they fuel him to work harder and dream bigger.

Chapter 25

Reading With Nanny Arlene

For many years, Port Arthur had three high schools. White students had attended Jefferson High on the eastern edge of Port Arthur, and black students had attended Lincoln High on the historic west side of town.

In August 2002, just before Jamaal starts tenth grade, there is major community news. Port Arthur's three high schools, Thomas Jefferson, Stephen F. Austin, and Abraham Lincoln, merge into one called Memorial High School.

This means big changes for everyone: teachers in new roles and students in new settings. For student-athletes like Jamaal, it also means more competition to make one of Memorial's sports teams. For instance, football players from Jefferson *and* Lincoln will have to make up just one varsity team.

Jamaal does not worry. He can see and feel the results of his extra conditioning. His confidence grows, and he cannot wait to show what he can do on the field and on the track.

With so many adjustments, Jamaal makes another important one. He starts a routine with his Nanny Arlene to practice, and improve, his reading. When he gets home from school, Jamaal heads to Nanny Arlene's bedroom and sits at the foot of her bed. He picks up the Bible and reads verses Nanny Arlene picks out in advance.

She reads the verse first.

"Isaiah 41:10," she says. "'So do not fear, for I am with you; do not be dismayed, for I am your God. I will strengthen you and help you; I will uphold you with my righteous right hand.'"

"Now you try, Jamaal," Nanny Arlene says.

Jamaal reads the verse aloud over and over again, asking for help when he gets stuck on a word. Nanny Arlene is gentle and patient with him. She never raises her voice. With her, Jamaal does not worry about misreading a word or asking a question. He trusts Nanny Arlene and knows she loves him.

After he finishes reading the verse, Jamaal and Nanny Arlene discuss the message and point of the verse.

"What does this mean?" Nanny Arlene asks.

"Not to be afraid because God is with me," Jamaal quickly says.

"That's right!" Nanny Arlene says. "What else?"

Jamaal pauses.

"Dismayed is the same as discouraged," he says, "and God wants me to know he will give me strength and help me."

Nanny Arlene gives Jamaal a high five.

They move on to another verse.

"'I can do all things through Christ who gives me strength,'" Nanny Arlene says slowly. "Philippians 4:13.

> I can do all things through Christ who gives me strength.
> Philippians 4:13

Now you try."

Each day, their goal is to finish one page in the Bible. Each day, Jamaal's confidence in reading grows. He concentrates on not skipping over letters or ignoring punctuation.

NANNY ARLENE'S RULE

"If you don't practice, you don't improve," Nanny Arlene tells Jamaal. "Hard work pays off."

Jamaal applies that same attitude at football practices.

The Memorial Titans head football coach is Coach Colbert. He coached at Thomas Jefferson. During one practice, the coaches discuss each player's position.

"Let's put Jamaal at cornerback," Coach Colbert says.

But running back coach Bubba disagrees.

"Coach, you got the wrong guy," Coach Bubba says. "Jamaal is not a corner. We need to get him the ball."

Coach Colbert decides to honor seniority. That means he gives preference to players who are older. James Johnson is a senior, and Jamaal is a sophomore.

Jamaal starts the football season as the third-string running back and main kickoff returner. At the beginning of a game or the second half, the opposing kicker boots the ball down field, and the kickoff returner tries to run the ball as close to the other end zone as possible. It's a position that requires a player who is fast and makes defenders miss tackles.

On the first play of the season, Jamaal gets to return a kickoff. The ball sails toward him at the 10-yard line, and he hauls it in and then sprints up the field. He sidesteps one defender and then turns toward the left sideline.

Two defenders tackle Jamaal, but he gains 42 yards to give his team momentum to start the game. In the second game of the season, the Titans dominate an opponent, and Jamaal hears his name.

"Get in there at running back, Jamaal," Coach Bubba says. "Show everybody what you can do."

Jamaal beams.

He pulls his helmet on, sprints to the huddle in the middle of the field, and awaits the play call from the quarterback. It's a counter run play, which means he'll fake one way then go the other. Jamaal *loves* that play.

The center snaps the ball to the quarterback, who hands the ball to Jamaal. As soon as he secures the ball, Jamaal takes a step right and plants, then he cuts hard to his left and explodes toward the left sideline.

Though three defenders are in position to tackle him, they just cannot get to Jamaal in time. To fans in the stands, it appears as if the defenders are moving at normal speed, and Jamaal is moving in fast forward.

He scores a 54-yard touchdown and no one touches him.

Coach Bubba walks next to Coach Colbert and puts his arm around him.

"Told you we need to get Jamaal the ball."

In the third game of the season, the Titans' opponent gets to return the opening kickoff. Jamaal is on the field, trying to use his speed to keep the return short. He hustles down the field, and he sees the other team's returner. As Jamaal approaches, the opposing player cuts hard to the right. Jamaal reaches back, and he grabs his jersey.

As they go to the ground, Jamaal's left finger twists and pops.

"Ouch, ouch!" Jamaal screams.

He winces in pain and grits his teeth. He cannot bend his left index finger: the one most people point with.

Coach Colbert and a doctor rush across the field to check on Jamaal.

The doctor softly checks different areas on Jamaal's left hand. Jamaal flinches each time.

"We'll need to get an X-ray," the doctor says, "but I believe he has a broken bone in his hand."

Jamaal panics. *When can I play football again? Will I ever be able to play again?*

Jamaal cries. But peace comes over Jamaal as he remembers the passage he read with Nanny Arlene. *I am not afraid,* he thinks, *because God will help me and give me strength.*

Chapter 26

The Spare Tire

Jamaal needs surgery to fix his finger. He is nervous. *How will they fix it? How much will it hurt? When can I play football again?*

Jamaal and his mom drive to Beaumont. The doctor at the hospital there explains everything kindly and clearly.

"Jamaal, during surgery you are not going to feel a thing," the doctor says. "After your surgery is done, you cannot play football the rest of this season. But, in a few months, your finger will be as good as new!"

After surgery, Jamaal gets a cast on his left hand. The cast is hard and protects his healing finger.

Jamaal cannot play football, but his uncle encourages him.

UNCLE ROBERT'S RULE

"Accept every outcome," Uncle Robert says, "and keep believing in yourself."

Jamaal does not want to be inactive, so he decides to join the cross country team. Cross country running is a long-distance race over natural terrain such as dirt, grass, or woodlands. Races usually cover three miles, which is 12 laps around a typical high school track.

The first time he runs with his new teammates, Jamaal tires after just one mile because his body is not used to running so far. But each week, he builds his endurance—the ability to push through fatigue and stress.

When it rains, Jamaal covers his cast with a plastic bag. Jamaal also flips tractor tires to improve his strength, and he practices his sprints and hurdles.

Danny and Cal pass by Jamaal on the track after football practice one Friday.

"I see you over there working," Danny says.

Jamaal smiles.

Jamaal and Danny become friends though they remain competitive with one another.

Before spring track tryouts, Jamaal walks up to Danny.

"I can beat you now," Jamaal says quietly.

"Come on, Jamaal," Danny says. "Are you crazy? Get out of my face with that nonsense."

All of their teammates laugh.

Jamaal doesn't move, doesn't smile.

"Are you serious?" Danny asks.

Jamaal nods.

Danny decides to give Jamaal a race.

"Let's do it in 20 minutes," Danny says.

Word spreads quickly.

Dozens of students and athletes, including football players, rush toward the track so they can watch Danny and Jamaal race in the 100-yard dash.

"Danny's going to win this race by at least four steps," one track teammate says to another.

"I say six," another adds.

Danny and Jamaal get into position and start the race clean. Usually, Danny pulls away after 20 meters, but Jamaal is step-for-step with him this time.

Danny gets a three-step lead after 50 yards, but Jamaal grows stronger because of the cross country running. He starts to close the lead as they near the finish line.

When they cross, Danny barely wins.

"Sheesh, that was only one step," an observer says. "Is Danny getting slower or Jamaal getting faster?"

When spring track starts, Jamaal does not make the four-man relay team again. He is the fifth-fastest sprinter.

Then Cedric Harris gets sick in an early meet against Beaumont and he cannot compete. Jamaal steps up. He and his teammates win the 4x100 and the 4x200. In the latter race, they shave

two seconds off the fastest time of the season.

Jamaal is the difference!

"We used a spare tire and ran that?" Coach Leopold says. "Someone is getting cut tomorrow." A *spare tire* is Coach Leopold's colorful way of saying a backup athlete.

Jamaal becomes one of the four top relay sprinters.

Coach Leopold notices that Jamaal works harder. He runs every race full speed. After practice, Jamaal leads younger athletes in drills to work on finishing races hard. Though everyone is already tired, Jamaal pushes himself and others to go an extra 20 minutes.

By the spring of his sophomore year, Jamaal has never felt stronger physically or mentally.

Chapter 27

Perfect Storm

Jamaal is fast and so are his teammates. But four fast runners are not enough to win relays.

Each team member must pass a baton within a 20-meter passing zone. Dropping the baton or making a pass outside the zone results in a disqualification. And having a slow handoff? That can cost a team precious time.

The best teams are fast and have precise timing, excellent skill, and technique.

And they practice a lot.

Jamaal, Culvin, Danny, and Valerious become the best in the region and state. They set the national record in the 4x200 relay!

Jamaal runs summer track and qualifies in the 400-meter hurdles for the 2002 National Junior Olympic Championship in Omaha, Nebraska.

Then another first: a flight.

He cannot drive from Port Arthur to Buffalo, New York. That's nearly 1,500 miles and would take almost 22 hours in a car. In a plane, though, they can cover that distance in three hours.

Where will I stay when I am away from home? Jamaal wonders.

Jamaal's family doesn't have money for plane tickets or hotel rooms. One of his youth coaches, Mr. Sinegal, helps to rally community leaders to pay for Jamaal's trip. Several people contribute, but Mr. Sinegal needs more. He approaches Dr. Kirk Williams, an emergency room doctor and businessman.

"You know I wouldn't come to you with nonsense," Mr. Sinegal says to Dr. Williams. "This is a once in a lifetime trip for Jamaal, and he's a great kid."

Dr. Williams writes a big check. Jamaal can go!

Still, Jamaal is afraid. He's never been on an airplane, and he does not know what to expect. Jamaal decides he must be brave. He wants to keep on competing and, hopefully, winning medals.

Jamaal sits next to the window, and fastens his seat belt. As the plane speeds along the runway, Jamaal feels a sensation as it tilts up and ascends into the air. Within minutes, the airport vehicles on the ground are getting smaller and smaller, until they look like little dots.

This isn't too bad, Jamaal thinks.

Before long, he adjusts his seat back, puts on his headphones, and falls asleep. He wakes up hours later as the plane starts its descent into Buffalo's airport.

After a meet in Buffalo, Jamaal heads to Sherbrooke, Canada, for the World Youth Championships. The meet is huge and features athletes from at least 36 countries.

This is incredible, Jamaal thinks. He meets runners from all over the world. He also wins international medals!

Jamaal wins a gold medal in the medley relay with athletes from other states as the Americans beat teams from Poland and Japan. He also wins a bronze medal in the 400-meter hurdle.

In Canada, he sees how big the world is outside Port Arthur and even Texas. He pictures many, many possibilities for his life.

I want to make it to the Olympics, he says to himself.

A few days after he returns home, Jamaal and a few friends head to the hospital. Informed of a visitor, Dr. Williams heads outside and walks up to the boys.

Jamaal does not initiate the conversation.

"Are you Jamaal Charles?" Dr. Williams asks.

"Yes, sir," Jamaal replies.

"You can call me Doc," Dr. Williams says. "I heard you did great on your trip. Congratulations!"

"Thank you, sir," Jamaal says. "I appreciate it, sir. I really appreciate it."

"It was my pleasure, Jamaal," Doc says. "Keep up the good work."

As track season gives way to football season, Coach Leopold gives Coach Colbert a message.

"Jamaal can run all day long," Coach Leopold says. "I remember him running 400 meters, a full lap around the track. Jamaal finishes first in practice with a respectable time of 49 seconds. But Jamaal comes to me and asks, 'Coach, can I run it again?'"

"I said, 'Sure, Jamaal. We'll do it again tomorrow.' But Jamaal looks at me funny and says, 'No, I want to run it again now.' He heads back to the starting line, and he shaves a full second and a half off his first run."

"That's just unheard of," Coach Leopold explains to Coach

Colbert. "He approaches every run, even in practice, like it's for a gold medal."

Coach Colbert quickly understands what Coach Leopold means.

As the starting running back, Jamaal finishes every run by sprinting to the opposite end zone. He does so whether the end zone is 10 yards away or 90!

Jamaal also shows off his speed and stamina every Monday when the football players run 48 40s.

The 40 represents the 40-yard dash. The 48 represents the number of dashes the athletes run. 48 is also the number of minutes in a high school football game. The athletes run 48 40s, so they have the stamina to stay strong through a game.

And they do this *after* practice!

For the preseason and entire season, Jamaal finishes in first place every single time. Once he finishes in a tie for first with his friend Danny.

In his first varsity start, Jamaal faces Smithson Valley, a high school north of San Antonio. Some teammates are nervous, but Jamaal is not. He finishes the game with over 100 rushing yards.

He tops that number in his second start too. The Titans start the season strong, and Jamaal begins to attract a lot of attention. Assistant coaches from college football programs stop by to ask about him.

"Colleges like what you're doing, Jamaal," Coach Colbert says. "Keep working hard!"

Really? I had not dreamed of going to college, Jamaal thinks. *Can I do this?*

Jamaal starts to get

letters from colleges at his Paw Paw's house. But one of his cousins tells him not to get his hopes up.

"Man, you will never go anywhere in life," his cousin says. "You're not smart enough for college!"

That comment just inspires Jamaal to work even harder. Nanny Arlene encourages him.

"Of course you are college material," Nanny Arlene says. "Look at your brother Shan and some of your cousins. Getting to play football in college is more than what you do on the field."

Jamaal knows *exactly* what his aunt is talking about.

He is comfortable on a field and on a track, but school has never been easy. How would he handle college-level classes? Would someone help him?

Chapter 28

SAT Testing

The 2003 football season is a blur for Jamaal. He finds his groove on the football field, posting dominant game after dominant game. He puts up crazy statistics, and people outside Port Arthur start to hear about him. He goes from an unknown player to a hot prospect attracting major college programs like Texas Christian University, Florida, Miami, and the University of South California.

At least 30 colleges were interested In offering Jamaal an athletic scholarship to play football, run track, or both! But three colleges intrigue him the most: the University of Florida, Texas A&M, and the University of Texas.

His heart was set on Florida because they had a great track team.

Oklahoma features a proud tradition in football, with seven national championships and five Heisman Trophy winners. The Heisman Trophy is given to the country's top college football player.

The University of Texas also has traditions and distinctions, such as its mascot Bevo, the Longhorn steer, wearing the colors burnt orange and white, flashing the Hook 'em Horns hand signal and singing loud fight songs. In 2002, Sports Illustrated selects the University of Texas as "America's Best Sports College."

One of the University of Texas assistant coaches watches one of Jamaal's games and insists on showing the video to his head coach.

"You gotta watch this young man," the assistant coach says.

Longhorns head coach Mack Brown is positive and popular. Once a running back at Vanderbilt and Florida State, Brown has built a strong reputation as a coach with stops at several big programs, including Oklahoma. Brown took over the University of Texas after establishing success with the football program at the University of North Carolina.

Nearly every boy who plays football in Texas—and throughout the region—dreams of becoming a Longhorn. Naturally, Coach Brown gets to pick the best of the best.

He is mesmerized by Jamaal.

Coach Brown sees a running back who explodes out of the backfield. Beyond the speed, Coach Brown also sees how well Jamaal avoids defenders.

"No one can touch him," Coach Brown says to his assistant coach. "He looks like a young Walter Payton."

That is a high compliment: some consider Payton the greatest running back in NFL history. Nicknamed "Sweetness," Payton starred for the Chicago Bears, leading them to a victory in Super Bowl XX and earning a spot in the Pro Football Hall of Fame.

Coach Brown tells his staff to do a background check on

Jamaal. That means Longhorn staffers will check Jamaal's grades and speak to his teachers, counselors, principals, and coaches.

One Saturday, hours before the Longhorns play a game, Jamaal visits the campus in Austin, Texas. The school is massive, just a quarter mile from the Texas State Capitol, and its colors and logos are everywhere: on flagpoles, cars, and even on the sides of buildings and houses.

Before the game, a Longhorn official gives Jamaal and his family a tour of the campus and athletic facilities. Then they head to the Darrell K. Royal-Texas Memorial Stadium. The stadium was originally built in 1924 and it seats over 80,000 people!

Before kickoff, Jamaal gets to stand on the field, and he scans the stands. It radiates a burnt orange glow.

After Texas wins the game, Jamaal and his Uncle Robert go inside the Longhorns' locker room. As players celebrate, they greet Jamaal warmly.

"I've heard about you!" one of the players says to Jamaal. "I hope you come here and help us win a national championship!"

Later, Jamaal, Nanny Arlene and Uncle Robert visit with Coach Brown. He is funny. He is warm. And he is straight forward.

"Everybody at your school says you are a sweet and hard-working young man," Coach Brown says. "I think you are Longhorn material. But you know what?"

Jamaal leans forward.

"You're going to have to do better in college than you did in high school on the field *and* off the field. That's hard to do," Coach Brown says. "But we'll give you all the resources to help you achieve those goals."

Coach Brown offers Jamaal an athletic scholarship.

Attending college was not even a dream for Jamaal until a few months ago!

But nothing can be official until Jamaal is a high school senior... and Jamaal must clear one last massive hurdle: the S.A.T.

The S.A.T. is a standardized test used for admission into colleges and universities in the United States. It tests reading, writing, and math skills. The score range is 400 to 1,600.

On the field during his senior year, Jamaal does not disappoint Coach Brown. Jamaal leads the Titans into the playoffs. Jamaal's teammates, especially his fullback and friend Cal, want to get him over 1,000 rushing yards. That means he needs 100 against Aldine High School.

But Aldine has three really good linebackers—the players who line up behind the defensive line.

On his first carry, Jamaal fumbles the ball, and an Aldine linebacker scoops it up and returns it for a touchdown. On the next series, the Titans' quarterback throws an interception. The Aldine Mustangs score another touchdown. Down 28–6 in the second quarter, Jamaal loses *another* fumble before halftime.

At halftime, the Titans' locker room is quiet. Cal, one of the team's captains, tries to fire up the players.

"Is this how we're going to act?" Cal asks loudly. "We can still win this thing!"

Cal walks up to Jamaal, who is sitting quietly by himself.

"You don't look like yourself, Jamaal," Cal says.

"Something don't feel right," Jamaal says.

Jamaal reaches into his bag and pulls out his old cleats. The game is played on a fancy surface called field turf. For the playoffs, the players receive new football shoes with cleats that screw in at the bottom.

Jamaal switches to his favorite football shoes which have molded cleats that cannot be replaced.

"Whatever you do," Cal tells Jamaal, "hold on to the football. We still have a chance!"

Jamaal gets the first handoff of the second half, and he blasts up the middle, sidesteps the safety, and scores a 70-yard touchdown.

The score is now 34–14, Mustangs.

The Mustangs punt after the next offensive series. Cal blocks a linebacker, and Jamaal squeezes between a linebacker and safety to find more space. He scores a 60-yard touchdown.

34–21, Mustangs.

The Mustangs offense cannot move the ball on the next series, and the Titans get the ball back. The Titans offense lines up with only Jamaal in the backfield. They look like they are throwing the ball. But the quarterback drops back, waits a moment, and hands the ball off to Jamaal.

He scores a 50-yard touchdown.

34–28.

Key pass defense by Danny forces another Mustangs punt. Jamaal pops another long touchdown run.

35–34, Titans.

Aldine rebounds and scores a touchdown on the next series. The Aldine kicker then misses the extra point, which is worth one point.

40–34, Mustangs.

Three minutes remain. Jamaal gets chunks of yards and moves the Titans down the field. But time is running out, and the Titans have the ball at the Mustangs' 4-yard line.

The play call comes from the coach to Cornelius, the quarterback. He fakes the handoff to Jamaal but keeps the ball. He takes a few more steps back, then he tosses the ball toward receiver Kelvin Jackson.

The ball descends and lands in Kelvin's arms. He secures it and scores! The Titans kick the extra point.

41–40, Titans!

In the second half, Jamaal racks up 300 rushing yards and four touchdowns. He is happy he switched shoes!

The Titans lose in the third-round of the playoffs after several injuries. It's the Titans deepest playoff run since the 1980s.

There's a nationwide buzz about Jamaal. He finishes the season with 2,051 rushing yards and 25 touchdowns. But Jamaal is especially proud because he wins the Willie Ray Smith award! That is the big award Shan did not get.

Football is getting easier and easier.

The S.A.T.? Well, that's another story. The test intimidates Jamaal; there are lots of confusing words and complex math problems.

Jamaal has months to practice, and can retake the test as many times as he wants. He has to earn a qualifying score before his offer from the Longhorns is official. First, though, he must take a practice test to see where he is at.

The test is long and takes hours to complete. Some of the questions are easy, some of them are hard. But when he is done, Jamaal just knows his head hurts.

Getting tackled by a defensive lineman is easier than the test!

The maximum score is 1,600, and Jamaal will need to earn at least 750 points. If he does not achieve his S.A.T. score mandate, he will have to consider other college options at smaller football programs.

Jamaal totals up his mock test. He does not score well. He takes a deep breath.

"That's just the first time. Don't worry about it," Uncle Robert tells Jamaal. "You have time to practice."

I have some work to do, Jamaal thinks.

Tae-Tae, a gifted basketball player, is also being recruited, so she and Jamaal study for the S.A.T. together. They study after school each night and for several hours on Saturday mornings. They sit at the dining room table and quiz one another... and take plenty of snack breaks.

Nanny Arlene and Uncle Robert are proud of how hard both of them are working. One Saturday, though, Jamaal gets a little frustrated when he scores 600 on a practice test.

NANNY ARLENE'S RULE

"Don't give up," Nanny Arlene tells Jamaal. "Keep practicing, keep trying."

Nanny Arlene continues to push and encourage Jamaal. So do his teammates, some of whom also get a chance to play football in college. Cal will play at Nicholls State University in Louisiana, while Danny will play at Texas A&M. They do not have any trouble getting the S.A.T. score they need and provide Jamaal some tips.

But Jamaal notices something as he puts in extra work on the S.A.T.: he's performing better in his classes.

Chapter 29

Facing Chopper

The spring of his junior year, Jamaal dominates in track. He is the state's best hurdler, consistently winning the 110- and 300-meter races.

After taking an S.A.T., Jamaal heads to a track meet. The hurdles and relays are already over, and there's only one race remaining. It's the 200-meter sprint, an event owned by Ivory "Chopper" Williams.

No one wants to even compete with Chopper, a native of Beaumont. At the 2002 U.S. Junior Championships, Chopper wins the 200-meter bronze medal.

Jamaal, though, is not afraid to lose. While it's not his usual event, Jamaal asks Coach Leopold if he can run the 200 anyway.

COACH LEOPOLD'S RULE

"When you want to be the best," Coach Leopold tells Jamaal, "you've got to beat the best."

Jamaal excels in the preliminary races and qualifies for the finals.

Chopper is a faster sprinter than Jamaal. But Jamaal hopes his conditioning will allow him to close the gap toward the end of the 200. As expected, Chopper bolts to an immediate lead on the entire field of athletes. But after 100 meters, Jamaal does not slow down. He pushes himself. He is, after all, fresh!

Jamaal closes in on Chopper, but he runs out of room and time. Chopper crosses the finish line before anyone else, including Jamaal, and wins the race. Jamaal finishes second. Not bad for his first time against this level of competition.

Jamaal wants the relay titles, and he wants Danny to compete with him. But Danny has already earned an athletic scholarship to Texas A&M to play football, and he does not want to run track.

"Man, we've got something special," Jamaal says to Danny. "We got that national record before. Now let's keep it going. Let's do it together."

Danny does not want to disappoint Jamaal. They are good friends, and he can tell this goal means a lot to Jamaal.

Memorial quickly asserts itself as the best in the state in all three relays: 4x100, 4x200 and 4x400. But at a major meet, Coach Leopold pushes Jamaal hard.

Nanny Arlene yells down to Coach Leopold.

"You're going to kill him!" she screams.

Jamaal will run the 110- and 300-meter hurdles, as well as the three relays.

"You don't have to run all of that," Coach Leopold tells Jamaal. "If you don't feel like you can do this, let me know so I can get someone ready."

Jamaal listens to his coach as he stretches on a corner of the track.

"Can you check with me a little later, Coach?" he asks politely.

About 10 minutes later, Coach Leopold checks in with Jamaal.

"Let me see something," Jamaal says.

He then runs and jumps over two hurdles.

"I'm ready, Coach," Jamaal says.

After that, Jamaal focuses on the three relays. At the state meet, Jamaal's team is heavily favored to win all of them.

While running the 4x100, Jamaal's calf feels strange, and he runs a slow second leg. The Titans finish fifth.

In the 4x200, Jamaal feels fine, but he does not run a fast time. The Titans finish third.

Then in the 4x400, Jamaal runs even worse. The Titans finish last out of eight teams.

"I'm sorry," Jamaal says to Danny.

"Are you kidding?" Danny says. "I'm the one who should be sorry. I could have run better all season and not put so much pressure on you."

They exchange a high-five. Jamaal is thankful for a friend like Danny.

In one of Memorial's final practices, Jamaal challenges Danny to one more race.

"I *know* I can beat you now," Jamaal says.

Danny laughs.

"You said that last time, remember?"

Jamaal remembers.

The two friends line up for a race. This time only their track teammates and coaches watch.

"Ready, set, go!"

Jamaal and Danny both start strong. But Danny does not pull away after 15 or 20 meters. They are tied halfway through the race then Jamaal seems to turn on another gear. Given his great conditioning, Jamaal pounds his legs harder and harder, and he pulls away from Danny.

Jamaal reaches the finish line two and a half steps before Danny. Jamaal wins!

"Good race, Jamaal," Danny says. "You finally got me!"

Jamaal smiles at his friend.

A few days later, Doc invites Danny and Jamaal over to his mansion for dinner. Doc wants to introduce them to someone. The boys play with Doc's children until a car pulls up. It's a super fancy car called a Bentley.

The man who steps out of the car is dressed very nicely, and he wears a big, shiny necklace.

Is that real? Jamaal wonders.

"This is Mr. Butler," Doc says to Jamaal and Danny.

The boys know who he is—a famous rapper!

But Mr. Butler gets serious.

"Look here. Y'all think this is something," Mr. Butler says, holding his very expensive necklace. "This isn't important." Mr. Butler explains some of the mistakes he's made and how older, wiser men like Doc help him.

MR. BUTLER'S RULE

"Do the right thing," Mr. Butler says, "and listen to those who come before you."

Chapter 30

Rising to the Occasion

After his breakout season in the fall, Jamaal remains the Titans' starting running back for spring football. He makes many lists as one of the nation's top senior running backs, and the Titans rank among Texas' top schools.

Jamaal does not rest on his accomplishments. He is the first to arrive at practice and the last to leave. The morning after games, he heads to the gym for a workout then watches film to see how he can improve.

During a spring practice, Jamaal awkwardly lands on his right shoulder.

In the past, he has felt his shoulder pop out, but it always quickly returns to normal. Not this time. He feels a shooting pain. And he cannot move his arm.

The team doctor checks on Jamaal and insists they will need additional tests.

The next day, Jamaal's nightmare becomes reality: He will need *another* surgery—and he'll miss a lot of time. There will be no summer track for Jamaal, and he will miss at least the first football game or two.

In the season opener, without Jamaal, the Titans lose. Big. They are blown out, 41–0.

In the second game, without Jamaal, the Titans lose to Tyler High School, 21–13.

The Titans start the season 0–2 then face Midland Lee High School, a three-time state championship football program. No one gives the Titans a chance to compete against the Lee High School Rebels, even with Jamaal back on the field.

The confidence of Jamaal's teammates is shaken. Coach Bubba pulls Jamaal aside.

"What makes you special," Coach Bubba tells him, "is that you shine against the average teams *and* the great teams."

COACH BUBBA'S RULE

"Embrace the big moments," Coach Bubba tells Jamaal. "The bigger the stage, the better you perform."

Can Jamaal, who hasn't played in months, make an impact like he did during the postseason?

To give his teammates confidence, the usually quiet Jamaal does something out of character. He publicizes his goal *before* the Midland Lee game.

"I'm going for 300 yards," Jamaal tells anyone who will listen.

That's a big number against a great team like the Rebels. They have at least six players who are going to play college football!

In the game, Jamaal seems to once again play at a different, faster speed than the other players. The Rebels cannot touch him, let alone tackle him. Jamaal's first carry goes for an 80-yard touchdown.

Because it is 100 degrees on the field, Coach Leopold worries that Jamaal may need some rest before the offense's next series.

"Son, you tired?" Coach Leopold asks Jamaal.

Jamaal makes a strange face.

"No, Coach," Jamaal says. "I'm good."

He's played in stifling heat most of his life.

The Titans hand the ball to Jamaal over and over again. In the third quarter, the Titans face a third down and 15.

"Let's throw the ball," Coach Leopold says.

But Coach Bubba has another idea.

"Are you kidding me?" he says. "Don't throw the ball. Hand the ball to Jamaal. He's got the hot hand!"

Jamaal runs the ball and gains 20 yards for another first down!

When the game is over, Jamaal has 49 carries and 371 yards. He blew away his goal of 300 rushing yards.

Unfortunately, the Rebels score a late touchdown and win 35–28.

🏈 **71yd**
🏈 **41yd**
🏈 **72yd**
🏈 **52yd**
🏈 **45yd**

"I just have to say I'm glad I don't have to play him again," Rebels coach Randy Quisenberry tells the Houston Chronicle. "He made it look so easy out there. We know we'll never face another back like Jamaal Charles."

Three games later, the Titans face Westfield High School.

Westfield fields at least 11 players who will play at major college football programs. Late in the game, Coach Bubba checks in with Jamaal on the sideline.

"You OK?"

"Yeah, Coach," Jamaal says. "It's just that I should have scored on the first play of the second half."

Coach Bubba thinks Jamaal is joking since he's already got four touchdowns. But Jamaal doesn't smile or laugh. Coach realizes that Jamaal is serious.

Jamaal goes off for 400 rushing yards and five touchdowns. The Titans win 48–41.

It's Westfield's only loss of the regular season, as they reach the state championship game.

During the season, Jamaal takes the S.A.T. test again. He gets a 620. The Longhorns still want to give Jamaal an athletic scholarship, but he needs to get the S.A.T. qualifying score of 750. Jamaal continues to practice his S.A.T. workbooks and study with his Nanny Arlene.

In football, Jamaal helps his team win six of the team's final seven games to qualify for the postseason. But the Titans lose a shootout (57–49) to Lamar High School.

Despite missing the first two games of the season, Jamaal finishes with 2,056 rushing yards and 25 touchdowns. Those dominating numbers help him eclipse Joe Washington's school record for rushing yards.

Jamaal earns lots of awards: First Team All-State by the Texas Sports Writers Association and the Associated Press for the second consecutive year. *Parade* magazine names him an All-American in football, and the Army All-American Bowl selects him to play in their big game.

He also claims state titles in the 110- and 300-meter hurdles.

But the most important honor is a second Willie Ray Smith award.

"Now I have two," Jamaal tells Shan. "One for me, and one for you."

Lots of family members are on hand to celebrate Jamaal's big award. A few of them doubted Jamaal, but he does not let that bother him. He decided long ago not to concern himself with what others think or say.

He never forgets one of Grandma's rules: "Don't listen to them. Listen to God."

Chapter 31

Party Time

After the Longhorns win the famous Rose Bowl, Coach Brown flies to Houston and drives to Port Arthur to visit Jamaal, his mom, Uncle Robert, Nanny Arlene, and Tae-Tae. The Longhorns running back coach and another assistant join Coach Brown.

Nanny Arlene makes baked chicken, mac and cheese, green beans, and rolls for dinner.

"I can tell you're a family man," Coach Brown tells Jamaal. "If you fumble in a game, you need someone to hug after the game."

Jamaal prefers the University of Florida. The Gators play in the exciting Southeastern Conference, and they have lots of excellent coaches and athletes. But it's an 11-hour drive and a two-hour flight from Houston.

Coach Brown explains that the University of Texas is just a four-hour drive from Port Arthur.

PARTY TIME

Jamaal decides that there are a lot of benefits of staying closer to home, especially so his family can go to most of his games.

After dinner, they watch some of Jamaal's season highlights and discuss tutors and specialists who will help him in college.

"Remember what I told you last time?" Coach Brown asks Jamaal.

Jamaal nods.

"I have to do better in college than I did in high school," Jamaal says, "on and off the field."

Coach Brown smiles.

"I'm going to do everything you ask me to do," Jamaal concludes.

Jamaal just needs to get that S.A.T. score to make everything official.

Can he do it?

After Coach Brown's visit, Jamaal takes another S.A.T. He gets a 700. That's an improvement, but he needs a 750. He takes S.A.T. prep classes and practices his S.A.T. workbooks. Jamaal refuses to let his Longhorn dream slip away!

After more studying, Jamaal tries another S.A.T. a month later.

One day, he arrives at Nanny Arlene and Uncle Robert's house. His mom is also there.

"What's going on?"

All the adults smile.

Nanny Arlene pulls out an envelope and unfolds it.

"You got a 770, Jamaal!" Nanny Arlene beams.

Jamaal does not cry. He smiles.

"I did it," Jamaal says. "I did it!"

To celebrate, they all head to Luby's Cafeteria in town. Jamaal usually gets a piece of fried fish and mac and cheese.

"Can I get two pieces of fish?" Jamaal asks.

"Of course!" Uncle Robert says. "Go ahead and get two."

The next morning, they call Coach Brown and tell him the good news.

Jamaal is *officially* going to be a Longhorn. Hook 'em Horns!

Chapter 32

Longhorn Dream

They make the four-hour drive from Port Arthur to Austin, staying mostly on Interstate 10. Jamaal rides in the back with his mom. Uncle Robert drives, and Nanny Arlene sits in the front passenger seat.

They drive over the Colorado River, and past downtown Austin. Then they see Darrell K. Royal–Texas Memorial Stadium, home of the Longhorns football team.

They cruise in and around campus: the Lyndon B. Johnson Presidential Library, the LBJ Fountain, and the Main Building. The latter is the centerpiece of the school's sprawling campus. It is 28 stories tall, with 56 bells at the top.

Jamaal has finally arrived. He is at the University of Texas, where he will start his journey as a Longhorn student-athlete.

After they check in to their hotel, Jamaal heads to a fancy steakhouse to meet other Longhorn recruits and their families.

The next morning, Jamaal undergoes a physical. Team doctors want to make sure each student-athlete is healthy and that no injuries need to be treated. Once he passes that, Jamaal heads to the equipment room. This is one of the moments he has been waiting for!

Chip Robertson is the equipment manager, and he hands Jamaal a bag of Nike gear: t-shirts, shorts, socks and shoes, all featuring the school's signature burnt orange color.

"After each workout," Chip tells Jamaal, "just put your clothes in the basket with your jersey number, and my staff will wash and fold them."

Jamaal's eyes light up. He figured he would have to wash his own workout clothes!

Then there are a series of personality and academic tests. The professors and counselors want to identify Jamaal's strengths and areas of concern so they can develop strategies to ensure Jamaal receives all the resources he needs to maximize how he learns.

Like many student-athletes, Jamaal plans to get a jumpstart by taking classes during the summer. That way, he can familiarize himself with campus, adjust to the difficulty of college classes, and transition into a workout routine.

That evening, all the freshmen recruits go to Coach Brown's house for dinner.

Coach Brown and his family want to get to know the young men better and meet their families. Coach Brown always invites a former Longhorn football player to address everyone. Tonight, a player gives a speech titled, "Things I would have done differently."

The former player shares lessons he learned and mistakes he made: not studying enough, not getting enough rest, and partying too much on the night before a game.

On Sunday morning, Uncle Robert, Nanny Arlene, and Jamaal's

mom pack up the car and prepare to drive back to Port Arthur.

"I am so, so proud of you," Mom says as she gives him a big hug.

Uncle Robert and Nanny Arlene also hug Jamaal.

"You made it," Uncle Robert says.

"We are so proud of you," Nanny Arlene adds.

When they pull away, Jamaal is all alone. But he is not afraid.

Epilogue

Freshmen like Jamaal who join a powerhouse program like Texas, coming off a Rose Bowl victory and a Top 5 ranking, do not typically play right away.

But Jamaal is not a typical freshman.

Longhorns offensive coordinator Greg Davis immediately recognizes Jamaal's rare combination of speed, instinct, and talent. He puts Jamaal on the field right away.

In his first collegiate game against Louisiana-Lafayette, Jamaal carries the ball 14 times for 135 yards and one touchdown. In his third game, he scores three touchdowns and gains nearly 200 yards against Rice. In his fifth game, against mighty Oklahoma, Jamaal outshines another highly-recruited Texas running back, Adrian Peterson. Jamaal finishes with 116 rushing yards and one touchdown in a 45-12 blowout of the Sooners.

Jamaal averages 7.4 yards per run. He finishes with 1,035 total yards and 13 touchdowns to help the Longhorns win the national championship. He is chosen as the Big 12 Conference's Offensive Freshman of the Year. In the spring, he runs track and earns All-American honors in four events: the 60-meter indoor, 100-meter outdoor, 200-meter outdoor, and 4×100-meter relay

outdoor. At the Big 12 championship, Jamaal wins the title with a time of 10.23 seconds in the 100-meter dash.

In the classroom, Jamaal is also not a typical freshman.

Jamaal learned from his big brother ShanDerrick to take his studies seriously. Shan broke Pro Football Hall of Fame running back Eric Dickerson's freshman rushing record at Southern Methodist University. A back injury derailed Shan's promising football career, but Shan graduated and works for the gas company now.

Though he struggled early in his education, Jamaal thrives at the University of Texas, where he makes the UT Athletics Director's Honor Roll and becomes an Academic All-American.

"At Texas, I had resources and tutors," Jamaal says. "I had people to help me understand. I worked really hard, and it felt so good to become an Academic All-American."

Coach Mack Brown tells his players they are required to stay in study hall before practices for their first two years in the program. As third-year students, they could skip study hall sessions if they maintained a certain grade point average.

Jamaal had the grades, but he elected to remain in the study hall.

"The thing that you want is for young men to have learned, gained confidence, had fun, and become successful," Coach Brown says. "For me, Jamaal is at the top of that list. Anytime there was a challenge, he met it with a positive attitude."

Others close to him agree with Coach Brown. Jamaal's positive attitude is one of his greatest assets. It helps him get through challenges and reach the many victories and milestones.

Before his second season starts, Jamaal spends a day with Doc and visits a part of Austin he'd never been to. They drive along Lake Travis, which features huge, gorgeous homes. They stop in the driveway of one house being built.

"This is where you can be," Doc tells Jamaal. "You've been blessed with abilities. Be humble, work hard, and one day you can have one of these."

As a junior, Jamaal finishes with 1,818 total yards and 18 touchdowns. Though he is a Heisman frontrunner, Jamaal decides to become a professional and enters the 2008 NFL Draft.

The NFL's 32 clubs select 252 players over seven different

rounds. The players selected earlier receive bigger contracts. On the first day, over two rounds, seven running backs are selected.

Jamaal is not among them. He cries.

"It was one of the hardest moments of my life," Jamaal says. "But God humbled me and it made me a better person."

Jamaal is the ninth running back drafted, as the Kansas City Chiefs select him in the third round. In the eight seasons since, Jamaal has established himself as one of the NFL's premier playmakers. Jamaal's friend Danny Gorrer played five seasons in the NFL

A four-time Pro Bowl selection, Jamaal owns a special NFL record: more yards per carry (5.5) than any other running back with at least 1,000 career carries.

Jamaal's professional career, however, hasn't been without its challenges. He's suffered three serious injuries, including two that required knee surgery. His latest knee injury occurred in the fifth game of the 2015 season. He returned for a few games in 2016, but he needed another minor surgery in November.

Jamaal wants his legacy to extend beyond football fields. His Jamaal Charles Youth Matters Family Foundation promotes the development of healthy minds and bodies and reinforces the motto that "Determination wins." He awards five scholarships annually to students with disabilities. The scholarships allow them to attend his alma mater, the University of Texas.

Jamaal also inspired thousands at the Opening Ceremony of the 2015 Special Olympics in Los Angeles by sharing his story of struggle and triumph.

"I was afraid. I was lost. I had trouble reading. I found out I had a learning disability," he said. "People made fun of me. They said I would never go anywhere. But I learned I can fly. The Special

Olympics gave me my first chance to discover a talent I did not know I had."

Cal Jones remains one of Jamaal's best friends.

"No one had to know about his struggles to learn," Cal says of Jamaal's speech. "But he wants to raise awareness and help kids who are struggling and may be ashamed like he was. It was courageous and a very selfless act."

Cal says Jamaal epitomizes the best of a young person dreaming and achieving.

"People said he would never be good at the hurdles because he was too clumsy, but he became a two-time state champion. People said he wasn't smart enough to play at the University of Texas, but he was an Academic All-American. People in high school said he was not a running back, but we watch him play on Sundays in the NFL

"There was so much negativity that surrounded him, but he overcame it all. He became more than anything any of us could have imagined, and he never took a short cut."

After graduating from Memorial High School, Jamaal speaks to the Port Arthur Community Chronicle about his plans—*to have my dreams come true, goals accomplished, my family surrounding me, and God forever in my life.*

Jamaal has been and remains a role model for Kenneth Lofton's children, and especially his son Geremiah, who had dyslexia.

"He motivated my son," Kenneth says. "He saw how hard Jamaal worked for everything."

Geremiah is a junior with a 3.6 grade point average at Huston-Tillotson University, where he is an all-conference track athlete and president of his fraternity.

When he became an NFL player, Jamaal bought his mom a

new home and car. In 2012, Jamaal married his college girlfriend, Whitney, and they have two daughters, Makaila and Makenzie.

In March 2017, Whitney and Jamaal will welcome a baby boy into the world.

Jamaal does not know how long he will play football. But he knows God has big plans for him afterward. He wants to share his story, along with the lessons and rules he's learned and implemented along the way.

JAMAAL'S LIFE RULE

"It's not easy to be successful. If you give up, you won't ever know how far you would have gotten. Everybody will have downfalls in life. But be thankful in your downfalls because that's what will make you stronger and make you want to be successful."